*Music in State Clothing*

THE LIFE GUARDS

# Music in State Clothing

## THE STORY OF THE KETTLEDRUMMERS, TRUMPETERS AND BAND OF THE LIFE GUARDS

G. R. Lawn

LEO COOPER

LONDON

First published in Great Britain in 1995 by
LEO COOPER
190 Shaftesbury Avenue, London WC2H 8JL
an imprint of
Pen & Sword Books Ltd,
47, Church Street, Barnsley, South Yorks, S70 2AS

ISBN 0 85052 454 7

A CIP record for this book is available from the British Library

Typeset by CentraCet Limited, Cambridge
Printed by Redwood Books Ltd, Trowbridge, Wilts

# Music in State Clothing

# List of Illustrations

*Colour Illustrations*     *Facing*

# Foreword

by

## SIR COLIN DAVIS

Those who remember the days with Colonel Lemoine in the Eton Country Club may jog their memories with this history of The Life Guards Band. The mixture of the ludicrous with the tedious, the scurrilous with the solemn, that was the life of a bandsman in those days will flood back into the memory as the water drowned the banks of the Thames in 1947. Musicians were not over comfortable with authority and thank God, it wasn't too much in evidence with Colonel Lemoine. Other musicians in other bands had a far worse time of it than me.

Here in this book is a portrait of The Life Guards Band from its inception, what they wore, how organized, who were the Music Directors, and their problems in peace and war. Anyone who spent a short time with them or made a career playing with them will find pleasure in this book, and will be grateful to G. R. Lawn for taking such infinite and detailed pains over the history of an institution that has given much pleasure to such a variety of people.

LONDON 1994

# Introduction and Acknowledgements

The history of a relatively small section of a regiment would on first thought seem unimportant with not much to record, multiply the small section by 334 years and the result is a catalogue of a wide variety of stories and events of the predecessors of one of the few remaining bands of the British Army.

The Life Guards have always been thought of as being different from other regiments and, as they are the senior regiment of the British Army, they probably are. Researching into the history of their band was certainly not as would have been expected with the seventeenth and eighteenth centuries being relatively simple while from the nineteen fifties to the present proved the most difficult period.

Help in my searches and pesterings came from many sources and I therefore offer my sincere thanks to the following: the late H. Sutherland, formerly 2nd L. G. Band; P. Allen; Lt–Colonel N. Bearcroft (Salvation Army); the late H. B. Dunsmore; I. D. Gunn; B. A. Harman; F. J. Harman; Major W. Jackson, MBE; E. G. Madden; Major J. G. McColl; R. McDonald; R. Newnham; Colonel A. J. Richards and K. R. Whitworth, all being former members of the Band of The Life Guards; CoH. O. N. Cook and BCM I. Graves of the Band; Miss Frances Dimond, curator of the photographic collection, Mrs Henrietta Ryan, deputy curator print room, Miss Jane Langton and Miss Elizabeth Cuthbert, former registrars, and Lady Miller, all of the Royal Archives Windsor Castle; Dr A. Ashbee; F/CoH. Chalmers, J. Cookson; Mrs Marjorie David; Miss Verity Davies of the *Neath & Port Talbot Guardian*; P. Faucet, former curator of the Royal Marines Museum; the late Mrs Marjorie Gleed, MBE, of the Royal Society of Musicians; R. J. Harris; R. Hutton; E. O. Lloyd, RVM; P. Mather; L. V. Shaw; E. Shilling; Major G. Turner, MBE; C. Waetzig; Mrs Gina Walker and RCM M. Whatley of the Household Cavalry Mounted Regiment. For permission to use

xiii

photographs thanks are due to H.M. The Queen, the Royal College of Music, the Royal Society of Musicians, Kingsley Jones of Windsor, Mrs Marjorie David, Patrick J. Stocks, LMPA, Paul Chave, Godfrey New, Godfrey Argent, David M. Bole, Clive Barda, The National Army Museum, H.Q. London District, *Soldier Magazine*, the Household Cavalry Museum and The Life Guards.

The Life Guards have been privileged to have had generations of many families serving the Regiment and the Sovereign, and generations of families have in turn been proud to serve. The Band have played no small part in the family of Life Guards, from the LeRagois, Grists, Rawlins and Winterbottoms to the Maddens, Dodsons, Harmans and Gooks of more recent years. Being myself of a Life Guards family, it is with great pleasure that I am able to record here my grateful thanks to those whose kindness and generosity has enabled this work to be published, many of whom have long family connections with the Regiment. J. H. A. Stillwell; L. M. Digby; Captain The Duke of Marlborough; The Life Guards Association; the Household Cavalry Charitable Fund; the Band of The Life Guards; Major T. R. S. Gooch, MBE; Major Sir J. Fuller, Bt; Captain M. Wyndham; Captain Lord Astor of Hever; Colonel W. H. Gerard Leigh, CVO, CBE; Flt Sgt G. A. Singleton; Colonel A. J. Richards; Lubbock Fine & Co. (Accountants); Dr R. G. L. Brittain; Major R. I. Ferguson; B. A. Harman; Major General Sir D. Langley, KCVO, MBE; Brigadier A. B. S. H. Gooch; C. T. Dean; Lt–Colonel S. E. M. Bradish Ellames OBE; Captain M. M. G. Naylor-Leyland, MC; Sir W. McAlpine, Bt; Major General Sir S. Cooper, KCVO; A. G. F. Fuller; J. P. Harrod; C. F. Corbett; Sir P. Naylor-Leyland; Major N. V. S. Paravicini, Dr C. Goodson-Wickes, MP and the WO's and NCO's Mess of the Household Cavalry Regiment and that of the Household Cavalry Mounted Regiment.

My special thanks to Major Tim Gooch, MBE, and Colonel Gerard Leigh, CVO, CBE, who took it upon themselves to spread the word; to Lt–Colonel A. D. Meakin, former curator; A. E. Woodbridge, former staff; Major A. W. (Paddy) Kersting, curator; A. P. A. Morris, assistant curator; all of the Household Cavalry Museum, and to Colonel G. McL. Stephen, OBE; Brigadier A. H. Parker Bowles, OBE; Colonel J. W. M. Ellery; Lt–Colonel P. S. W. F. Falkner; Lord Fanshawe of Richmond; Major G. G. E. Stibbe and L/CoH D. M. Bole of the Band. Also to Sir Colin Davis for his Foreword.

My very special thanks to Cherrie for her months at the word processor and without whom this book could have been written but with far fewer punctuation marks and some words spelt rong.

# CHAPTER 1

# The Troops of Horse Guards
# and Horse Grenadier Guards

The Band of The Life Guards is a title that first appeared in 1928, but the story of this famous band reaches back to 29 May, 1660, when on his restoration King Charles II made his public entry into London escorted by the King's Troop of Life Guards in three divisions, each led by its own kettledrummer and trumpeters.

On 26 January, 1661, King Charles formally established 'His Majesties Own Troope of Guards, His Highness Royall the Duke of York his Troope of Guards and His Grace the Duke of Albermarle his Troope of Guards'. Each troop had on its establishment four trumpeters and one kettledrummer each paid £91 per annum and each holding a warrant of appointment from the King. Later, on 2 April, 1661, a troop was raised in Scotland, its title, His Majesties Troope of Guards. The pay of this troop was lower than its English counterparts with a trumpeter receiving 2/8d and the kettledrummer 3/- per diem, being £48-13-4d and £54-15-0d per annum; all of these troops were sometimes called Guards, Horse Guards or Life Guards. From the formation of these troops no colour was specified for horses until 1685, when an order prescribed white horses for trumpeters of the Life Guards on state occasions.

Some of the musicians, if not all, held dual appointments, as a paper in the Lord Chamberlain's records of 1690 shows:- 'Certificate allowing Robert Mawgridge His Majesties Drummer in ordinary to continue the office of kettledrummer to His Majesties Troop of Horse Guards, He providing a sufficient man to perform the duty in his place of drummer.'

It is known that, of a list of trumpeters in ordinary to the King of September, 1689, all were at some time in the Troops of Horse Guards and in fact eleven* were so at the date of the list.

William Bull*  
John Stephenson*  
Thomas Barwick*  
John Segnior*  
Jervace Walker*  
William Shore*  
Hendrick Davant*  
Robert Maugridge K/D*  

Anthony Ragways*  
Daniel LeFever*  
John Doorescourt  
Bernard Van Batem  
Francis Giddins  
Richard Marsh*  
Christian Perll  
Nicholas Dewell  

To further confuse the issue a proposal in March, 1668, to lessen the cost of the Royal Household noted that the pay of seventeen trumpeters and a kettledrummer amounts to £1290, with eleven put into the Guards and their salaries of £60 each deducted, £660 will be saved.

The duties of the trumpeters and kettledrummers over the next 127 years made full use of their dual role as military and court musicians. Whitehall guards with a strength at this time of three officers, two trumpeters and one hundred private gentlemen, escorts, state occasions such as coronations, and the campaigns in Flanders were the bulk of their military duties, while frequent trips abroad attending the King, his Ambassadors and nobility were part of their court duties. One such journey was made on 9 June, 1677, to Poland by John Christmas of the Queens (2nd) Troop and Albion Thompson of the Kings (1st) Troop, attending the Right Honourable Laurence Hyde, Ambassador to the King of Poland. The unfortunate Trumpeter Christmas was killed shortly after arriving in Poland and on 20 October, by command of the King, a warrant was issued by the Lord Chamberlain giving Mrs Sarah Christmas, widow, £200 for herself and child.

Other casualties among the musicians were mainly instrumental, particularly trumpets which had a habit of getting lost, stolen or simply worn out.

'24th January 1675/6 Lord Chamberlain to Jewel House.
Whereas his Grace the Duke of Monmouth hath informed mee that one of his Majesties silver trumpetts in the custody of Symon Beale, one of his Majesties trumpeters, was lately lost and stole from off the Horse Guards and cannot be heard of, and that there is a trumpet wanting for his Majesties service; this is to require J.H. to prepare and deliver to Symon Beale one silver trumpet of the same fashion, quantity and proportion as any of his Majesties trumpets.'

*Kettledrummer First Life Guards.* Watercolour by A. I. Sauerweid 1816

Trumpeter First Life Guards 1828

The Garter Procession 1962

'27th January 1693/4 Lord Chamberlain to Jewel House.
Warrant to supply one new silver trumpet to William Shore, trumpeter to his Majesties 1st Troop of Horse Guards, being robbed of his trumpet this last campaign in Flanders, as is certified by the Earl of Scarborough.' William Shore took delivery of his new trumpet complete with crook and mouthpiece which in total weighed 36 oz 1 dwt on 2 March, 1694, the cost £20.

New kettledrums with all things necessary were made in 1675 by the King's brazier, John Revett, for the Queen's Troop, and in 1682 another pair were made to replace those lost at sea when the frigate *Gloucester* went down off Yarmouth; among those drowned was Kettledrummer Walter Van Bright of the Guards. The cost of these drums was £15 a pair inclusive of heads, sticks and spanners or £12 a pair for drums only. New drums for the 1st and 3rd Troops were made in 1690/1, for the 1st Troop again in 1703 and for the 3rd Troop in 1710. In 1713/4 the 1st Troop again had new drums, the cost this time being £14 a pair.

On the death of the Duke of Albermarle in 1670, his Troop, which had ranked third in seniority, became the Queen's Troop and was renumbered as the 2nd Troop, the Duke of Yorks (2nd) Troop becoming the 3rd Troop. The trumpeters and kettledrummers in the Troops on 10 April 1689 were:-

| *1st Troop* | *2nd Troop* | *3rd Troop* |
|---|---|---|
| Mr Maugridge K/D | Mr Brabant K/D | Mr Vandenand K/D |
| Mr Shore | Mr Bull | Mr Seinior |
| Mr Ragway | Mr Barwick | Mr LaFavour |
| Mr Marsh | Mr Stephenson | Mr Davant |
| Mr Keys | Mr John Shore | Mr Walker |

A 4th Troop of Horse Guards had been raised in England in 1686 but disbanded the following year and a troop of Dutch Guards became the 4th Troop in 1689. This 4th (Dutch) Troop was disbanded in 1699 and in 1709 the Scots Troop was numbered as the 4th Troop.

The personnel on 15 April, 1692, including the Dutch Troop were:-

| *1st Troop* | *2nd Troop* |
|---|---|
| Robert Mawgridge K/D | Francis Hemrick Kister K/D |
| William Shore | John Stephenson |
| Anthony Ragway | John Brookes |
| Francis Giddins | John Godfreid Ernst |
| Jo Williams | John Conrad Richter |

| 3rd Troop | 4th Troop |
|---|---|
| Cornelius Vandinande K/D | John Bullaert K/D |
| John Senior | John Dorscott |
| Jervase Walker | Christian Pearle |
| Daniell LeFever | Bernard Van Barton |
| Henrick Devant | Nicholas De Witt |

As can be seen from the names many of the musicians were Dutch, though some names in a short time became anglicised, for example John Senior, whose father had been in the Horse Guards as John Seignier. Anthony Ragway's father was Benigne LeRagois. There were many petitions and legal proceedings at this time.

> '21st May 1679
> Petition of Melque Goldt, setting forth that he served as a trumpeter in His Majesties Troop of Guards ever since His Majesties Happy restoration till last November, when he was dismist for being a Roman Catholique and having had no allowance since November is become so very poor, he cannot go into Suabia his native country, without some reliefe, there is £75 due to him out of the fee-farm and rents, £60 upon the law bill, and half a years sallary out of the treasury chamber, he £30, and he prays his Majesty to allow him wherewith to carry him home. The Petition is referred to the Duke of Monmouth, his just demands to be satisfied.'

> '23rd April 1694
> Whereas William Bull, Trumpeter, petitioned me to take his Course at Law against Robert Maugridge, Kettle Drummer, for scandalous words, and it being a matter to be decided at Law, I do hereby order ye Robert Maugridge to give an appearance to ye suit of Will Bull by ye first day of this Easter term, otherwise ye petitioner hath his liberty to proceed at Law against him.'

The dawning of the eighteenth century saw little change of any note in the establishment and duties of the Troops of Horse Guards. Several trumpeters were present at battles abroad in the appointment of Trumpeter to the Duke of Marlborough. One of these was Cornelius Vandenande who accompanied His Grace to Flanders in 1704. Another was John Conrad Richter of the 2nd Troop who went to Flanders in 1704/5, while 1706 John Senior of the 3rd Troop was present at the Battle of Ramillies, and two more went with the Duke to Holland in 1708.

A battle of a different kind took place in 1719 and was reported in the *Weekly Post* of 19 September:-

'On Sunday night last, Mr Darvin the famous trumpeter of the 1st Troop of Guards fought a duel at the Red Cow, behind St Clements, in which he received three wounds, two in the breast seven inches each, and one in the belly ten inches, yet they are not supposed to be mortal.'

Trumpets were still suffering, as warrants from the Lord Chamberlain to the Jewel House show.

'12th February 1717/18
Whereas the Earl of Hertford has certified that Mr Godfrey one of the trumpeters in the 2nd Troop of Horse Guards has broken his trumpet in a party last summer attending His Majesty in person. Warrant for a new trumpet.'

'12th February 1717/18
Whereas the Duke of Montague has certified that John Sheppard and Benj. Gossett, trumpeters in His Majesties 1st Troop of Horse Guards, are forced to make use of brass trumpets upon duty, their silver ones being broke and battered with nineteen years use that they are unservicable. Warrant for new trumpets.'

'20th May 1718
Whereas Lord Newburgh has certified that a silver trumpet belonging to His Majesties 3rd Troop of Horse Guards is broke and wore out. Warrant to provide and deliver to John Senior, trumpeter in the said troop, a new silver trumpet.'

Versatility was evident when, in 1739, John Jones of the Horse Guards, on joining the Royal Society of Musicians, gave his instrument as violin, which he later played as a member of the King's Band.

The Life Guards' first battle honour was gained in 1743 at the Battle of Dettingen in which several trumpeters and kettledrummers took part, their pay at the time was 5/- per diem. Three years later, in 1746, the 3rd and 4th Troops of Horse Guards were disbanded and their banners and kettledrums received into the Great Wardrobe.

By 1750 the 1st Troop had some negro trumpeters, possibly from as early as 1720.

Two of the most prominent musicians of the day were Valentine Snow and Kettledrummer Redmond (Radman) Simpson, who were both in the 1st Troop of Horse Guards. The latter became a member of the Queen's Band and of the Royal Society of Musicians, to whom he presented several portraits of other prominent musicians which are still in their possession. Kettledrummer Simpson is buried in Westminster Abbey. Valentine Snow became Sergeant Trumpeter to the King in 1753; he also was in the Royal Society. Another member of this society, G.F. Handel, is said to have written trumpet parts in 'Atalanta' for Snow in 1736.

In 1678 there was added to each troop of Horse Guards a division of Horse Grenadier Guards, each including on its establishment two hautbois. The King's Troop also had two drummers. The hautbois was an early form of oboe, and the drummers played on large brass-shelled side drums, both mounted and on foot. In January, 1680, the Horse Grenadiers were disbanded but were raised again in 1684 with an increase of hautbois to four per troop and two drummers to each troop except the fourth troop, which appeared to have had only two hautbois and two drummers.

> Lord Chamberlain to Jewel House
> '6th September 1686
> Warrant to provide liveries, drums and fittings for four trumpeters and a kettledrummer, with two drummers coats and two haut-boy's coats, in the Fourth Troop of Guards commanded by Lord Dover.'

> '29th September 1686
> Warrant to provide liveries for twelve hautboyes and six drummers for the 1st, 2nd and 3rd Troops of Guards, to be made ready against His Majesty's birthday and to be delivered to Capt. Ogilthorpe.

The three divisions of Grenadiers were amalgamated into an independant troop in 1693 which included on its establishment six hautbois, four drummers and a kettledrummer.

> '13th March 1694 Lord Chamberlain to Great Wardrobe.
> Warrant to provide liveries for a kettle-drummer, four drummers and six hautboyes in the Grenadier Guards commanded by Geo. Cholmondley.'

In 1702 a troop was raised in Edinburgh and attached to the Scots Troop of Horse Guards. This troop's establishment included four hautbois and four drummers. In 1709 the Scots Troop of Horse Grenadier Guards was renamed the 2nd Troop of Horse Grenadier Guards and their drums had the badge of the troop in *repoussé*, an example of which is in the National

Army Museum, London. Most certainly the 1st Troop would have had their badge in similar work. At the time of the funeral of Queen Anne in 1714 each troop had only four hautbois and four drummers, a kettledrummer no longer being on the establishment.

At the proclamation of the accession of King George III the order of procession began with:-

'Farriers of the Horse Grenadier Guards with axes erect
French Horns of the Regiment
Troop of Horse Grenadier Guards'

The term hautbois, originally used to denote hautbois players, had by the mid-eighteenth century fallen into use in the Horse Grenadier Guards as the title for any musician other than drummer. There is no one with the title of Horn in the 1760 muster roll, but by April, 1761, the term Horn was in use. Several players on the roll as Hautbois later appear as Horn and even Trumpeter, and later still Musician, as do some drummers. The Rank of Hautbois was finally abolished in 1775 when the hautbois and drummers were taken off the establishment and four trumpeters added in their stead. Further proof of the versatility of the musicians in the Troops of Life guards and Horse Grenadier Guards is Trumpeters Thompson, Denman and Purney, all of whom were members of the Royal Society of Musicians. On their admission to the Society their details were:-

Robert Thompson admitted 2nd April 1780. 'Is a trumpet in the Second Troop of Life Guards ... performs on the hautbois and clarinet'.
Edmund Denman admitted 4th April 1784. 'Is in the First Troop of Grenadier Guards plays the bassoon, clarinet and french horn.'
Laserre Purney admitted 3rd February 1788. 'Is one of the Trumpeters in the First Troop of Life Guards, he plays the trumpet, clarinet, violin and tenor.' Purney was soon to become kettledrummer of the First Regiment and later hold the same appointment in the Second Regiment.

It is quite possible that small bands of music were formed, with the players doubling on a variety of instruments.

The Horse Grenadier Guards continued in existence until 1788 when they played an important part in the formation of the Regiments of Life Guards.

CHAPTER 2

# Bands of Music of the
# Regiments of Life Guards

In 1788 a Royal Proclamation completely changed the structure of the
Troops of Horse Guards and Horse Grenadier Guards.

'GEORGE R.
Whereas we have thought fit to order our First Troop of Horse
Guards, commanded by our right trusty and entirely beloved cousin,
Lieut. General William Marquis of Lothian and our Second Troop of
Horse Guards, commanded by our right trusty and well-beloved
counsellor General Jeffery Lord Amherst, to be completely formed
into Regiments of Life Guards, and their Establishments and Pay as
such to commence the 25th June 1788; whereas it is become necessary, by the said Troops being formed into Regiments of Life Guards,
that their former titles as Troops of Horse Guards should be altered
and their future rank ascertained.

'Our Royal Will and Pleasure is that our First Troop of Horse
Guards, now under the command of Lieut. General the Marquis of
Lothian, shall bear the title of our First Regiment of Life Guards, and
our Second Troop of Horse Guards now under the command of
General Lord Amherst, the title of our Second Regiment of Life
Guards, and shall have the same precedence respectively in our
service which they now hold as Troops of Horse Guards. Whereof
the Colonels for the time being of our said Regiments of Life Guards
and all others whom it may or shall concern to take notice and govern
themselves accordingly.

Given at our court of Saint James this 8th day of June, 1788, in the
twenty-eighth year of our reign.
By His Majesty's Command
(signed) GEO. YONGE'

The establishment of each regiment included four trumpeters and a kettledrummer, each paid 2/6 a day. No mention is made in the establishment of hand musicians, but one, Michael Schreiber, a German aged 25, enlisted into the First Life Guards as a musician on 4 September, 1788, and was not appointed trumpeter until 4 May, 1793. For many years the appointment of trumpeter was the more important position in the regiments and this does appear to indicate that there was a band at this time. The earliest mention of bands is in the orders of the First Regiment of 16 March, 1795, 'The music of each Regiment will attend instead of the two trumpeters as was at first ordered'. Later that year musicians were being mentioned in orders as "extra music"

'17th August 1795
The following to be the distribution of Artificers and the public duty men belonging to the Regiment in order to equalize the troops.

| | | |
|---|---|---|
| Watson | (*Clerk*) | |
| Stock | (*Rough Rider*) | Capt. William's Troop |
| Ogden | (*Rough Rider*) | |
| Cooper | (*Extra Music*) | Capt. Shelly's Troop' |

The practice of musicians being allotted to troops or squadrons continued until 1922 when the Band became an independent unit within the Regiment.

Detachments of both regiments of Life Guards with their respective bands attended at the Palace of St James on the evening of the 8 April, 1795, when the marriage of His Highness the Prince of Wales with the Princess Caroline of Brunswick was solemnized. On 17 May, 1797, detachments of both Regiments, with their bands of music, again attended at St James's Palace on the occasion of the marriage of Charlotta Augusta Matilda the Princess Royal and the Duke of Wurtemberg.

During September, 1799, the trumpeters and kettledrummers of the Life Guards who held warrants were taken off the strength of the regiments but continued upon the Household establishment, kettledrummers and trumpeters, attested soldiers, who were to receive the pay of 2/6d per day, with the same allowance as rank and file, were placed upon the establishment of each regiment. On 2 December, 1799, a Trumpet Major was added to the establishment of the 2nd Life Guards, possibly because there was now no direct musical authority over the trumpeters as they were no longer under the direct authority of the Sergeant Trumpeter of the Royal Household.

The trumpeters of 1799 must have been good-hearted and easy-going men. A Second Life Guards order 20 June states:-

'The Trumpeters are not to ride their Regimental Horses on the road or for pleasure without leave, still less to lend them'.

They also lacked some discipline in 1803, 'when an example was made of a Musician for a most daring outrage, taking his pistols out of his quarters without leave, loading it in a house, and threatening unarmed inhabitants more like a footpad than a soldier'.

The orders of the First Regiment show that on 1 December, 1802, musicians were still extra music.

'The men will be settled with on 24th of this month for the amount of old Hats and Clothing which has been sold, after deducting the expenses attending the sale. To which will be added the proceeds of the Lace and the Old Furniture sold in like manner.

All the men who were in the Regiment on 31st March 1802, are to share, including those subsequently discharged. The Farriers and extra music are to share, but not the Trumpeters, who will have the velvet clothing in lieu when it is condemned.'

In 1810 a Trumpet Major appeared on the roll of the 1st Life Guards for the first time, though it is likely that one was appointed in 1799 as was done in the 2nd Regiment. Almost half of the trumpeters enlisting into the First Regiment at this time were Germans with one or two Dutchmen. On 25 December, 1810, the youngest and shortest Life Guard enlisted, Robert Jones, aged eight and three feet, eleven inches tall.

For the Peninsular campaign of 1812 both Regiments set sail. Among their number were Trumpeters James Rathbone, John Vanderwalker and Thomas Grist of the Firsts and Thomas Berwick, Charles Harris, Isaac Perks, John Perks (died), George Procter and Thomas Procter of the Seconds.

At the Battle of Waterloo Trumpeter John Edwards of the First Life Guards, as field trumpeter to Lord Edward Somerset, sounded the call for the decisive charge of the Life Guards. Also present at the battle were Trumpeters Joseph Freck and Jacob Lieber with their comrades of the Second Regiment Thomas Berwick, Charles Harris, Robert Mills and James Taylor, who was killed. The bugle used by John Edwards, a young man of nineteen, is in the Household Cavalry Museum at Windsor. In cavalry regiments bugles were used for field calls when mounted and trumpets when on foot.

A parade state of a review of the First Life Guards on 21 July, 1820, shows nine trumpeters on parade. Barely a fortnight later, on 5 August, there were twenty-two, which may indicate the extra music being referred to as trumpeters. If one allows for a colonel's trumpeter and four squadron trumpeters, this would leave seventeen, which, if on parade as a band, was numerically strong for this period and must have been satisfying for the Music Master, possibly Herr Bies. Two years later, at a review by the Duke of York, the parade state included twenty 'musicians'. About this time an attempt to train a negro kettledrummer failed when Josiah Uzabb of Martinique (Complexion Black) had to be discharged, in consequence of his not being able to learn to beat the drum. A little later the Second Life Guards had four negro trombone players. Two extracts from the 1st Life Guards standing orders of 1827 give some insight into the work of the trumpeters and music and the relative importance of horses and band engagements:

Article II 'Trumpeters are to be practiced twice a day until perfect, and the band at such hours as shall be approved by the Commanding Officer.' Article III 'The trumpeters and musicians are to take care of their own horses. Should any application be made for the band at any hour that interferes with stable duty, it cannot be granted, unless an arrangement can be made for the care of their horses.'

The Colonel of the Second Life Guards in 1830 was Earl Cathcart who, when Minister Plenipotentiary to St Petersburg, was most impressed with the Band of the Emperor's Imperial Guards, playing new chromatic brass instruments. The Czar, on hearing of his appreciation, presented a set for his regiment on condition the mechanism remained covered. Was this the origin of the leather covers of today? For many years a story has been circulating that the 2nd Life Guards were the first band in the British Army to have circular bass tubas. There appears to be no evidence to support this. During the latter part of the nineteenth century and early part of the twentieth century the First Regiment had two but, the Second Regiment used the standard tuba.

Less than a year after receiving their Russian instruments the Second Life Guards were presented with new silver kettledrums on 6 May, 1831, by King William IV at the Little or Home Park, Windsor. The magnificent drums weigh 118½ lbs and cost £980, with boxes for the drums costing

£20. They were made by Mr Key of Charing Cross. At the ceremony the now famous Russian chromatic trumpet band of the Regiment were part of a splendid occasion. Later, in the evening, the officers of the Regiment dined with His Majesty in St George's Hall. The silver kettledrums and standards of the Regiment were decorated with laurel and placed in the centre of the hall, immediately behind the King's seat. The Band of the Regiment played in one of the galleries.

Two months later, on 23 July, a similar ceremony took place when the King presented an identical pair of kettledrums to the First Life Guards and again His Majesty entertained the officers in the evening. In a report of the ceremony in the *Windsor and Eton Express* is one of the earliest, although misplaced, references calling a Life Guard Trumpeter a State Trumpeter. On this occasion he was the Trumpeter of the escort.

The King's birthday in 1833 was celebrated with a fête at Windsor Castle given by His Majesty. The Band of the Second Life Guards were part of the celebrations, playing in the orchestra in St George's Hall.

The Band of the First Regiment in December, 1834, marched from Windsor to Brighton with B, C, H and E troops and Regimental Headquarters. What the reason was is not clear, but, in 1830, the Second Regiment had marched to Brighton for riot duties.

When in London both Life Guards bands played regularly in Kensington Gardens on Tuesdays and Wednesdays. Richard Doyle's Journal of 1840 ably expresses public opinion:-

> 'I don't understand the meaning of this. Here the officers of the Blues have taken it into their heads to prevent the band playing in the Gardens on Tuesdays and Wednesdays. There was a general changing of barracks about a fortnight ago, the Life Guards who were here going to Windsor, those that were at Windsor coming to the Regents Park and the Blues who were there going to the Knightsbridge Barracks and when they got there refusing to do what both Regiments of Life Guards have always done and what they themselves always did other years when it came to their turn'.

Sometimes for Kensington Gardens concerts the First Life Guards band would only use mounted band instrumentation which, at the time, excluded woodwind. This also excluded the need for music stands which were usually transported by cart. This must have been very unpopular with the drummers who would have had to carry the cumbersome kettledrums. The brass players had music lyres attached to their instruments but obviously lyres were not yet available for woodwind instruments. Much to the disgust of the audiences only marches were played by this combination.

A letter from the Adjutant General to the Marquess of Londonderry, Colonel of the Second Life Guards, dated 22 May, 1845, is rather surprising when one considers the financial status required in those days to be an officer in the Life Guards.

'My Lord

I have had the honor to receive, and to submit to the Commander in Chief, Your Lordships letter of the present date, with its enclosures:-

His Grace commands me to refer your Lordship and to request, that your Lordship will be pleased to refer Colonel Reid to Article 107 on the interior management and economy of a Regiment, Page 138 and 139 of the Queen's Regulations and Orders for the Army, whereby it will be seen that Her Majesty considers 'the formation of a band of music upon an economical scale essential to the credit and appearance of a Regiment' and orders that every officer (married or single) on entering a Regiment, is to pay towards the maintenance and support of a Band, the amount of Subscription and annual contribution referred to in the official Memorandum herewith returned.

His Grace was aware, when that memorandum was issued, that the Officers of the 2nd Regiment of Life Guards had not, theretofore, subscribed to the Regimental Band, but nevertheless, considers it expedient, that they should, in this respect, be, for the future, placed upon the same footing as the other Officers of the Army.

John Macdonald. A.G.'

The first Grand Military Concert held in Great Britain took place at the Crystal Palace in June, 1851, when the massed bands of the Household Cavalry, Royal Artillery and Foot guards performed. The pieces were selected and conducted by the respective Bandmasters. The contributions of Bandmaster Waddell of the First Life Guards were his own arrangements of classical pieces, the others being of the popular type of the day. Newspapers of the time mention Waddell's arrangement of the overture to 'Euryanthe' as being the best piece performed.

At the funeral of the Duke of Wellington in 1852 the Band of the first Life Guards, with heart-thrilling strains of plaintive music, received special mention in the press; 'As while most of the bands played only the "Dead March in Saul" Mr Waddell's musicians played the funeral March from Mendelssohn's "Antigone" and a movement from Spohr's "Power of Sound Symphony" in addition to Handel's immortal march.'

When the highly esteemed Master of the Band James Waddell retired in 1863, Band Corporal of Horse James Waterson was appointed in his place and eventually enjoyed a reputation the equal of Waddell's. Two years after his appointment Waterson was promoted to the newly authorized rank of Bandmaster Corporal. With the responsibilities and authority of the Bandmaster now backed up by rank, the duties and responsibilities of the Trumpet Major were clearly defined in the 1856 Standing Orders of the Second Life Guards.

'Trumpet Major
The Trumpet Major ranks as a corporal and is placed in authority over the Trumpeters. It is his duty to instruct them, and he will be held responsible that they are efficient in all the Regulation sounds, for the Duty and Exercise of the Cavalry, a copy of which he must have in his possession.

'The supernumerary Trumpeters will attend practice for one hour daily, under his instruction, until dismissed.

'He will keep a roster and warn the Trumpeters for all duties which they may be required to mount; and is answerable that the Trumpeter on Piquet is made acquainted with the exact time at which he is to sound the various calls during his tour of duty.

'He has charge of the silver trumpets belonging to the Regiment, and will not allow them to remain longer out of his possession than is obsolutely necessary for the purpose of duty. The State Clothing is kept in the Regimental Store, and the Trumpet Major is responsible for its being issued to any of the Trumpeters or Band, for the purpose of duty, half an hour before the Trumpet sounds "To Horse" also, that it is collected and returned to the Regimental Store immediately the duty has been performed.

'In the absence of the Bandmaster, he has charge of the Band and will at all times exert himself in promoting the regularity and efficiency of the Musicians.

'He will make out Applications for Leave for any of the Band who require it, which he will submit to the Bandmaster for his signature previous to its being shewn to the Commanding Officer at the Orderly hour; and he will be held responsible that no application from any Musician is forwarded for permission to play at any disreputable or improper place.

'He will keep a Book in which he will enter all trifling offences and irregularities committed by the Band, which he will lay before the Adjutant for his decision.

'The whole of the Trumpeters are to assemble to sound for General Parade and Watch-setting. The Last Post at Watch-setting will be sounded at 8 minutes past 10 o'clock.

'When the Regiment changes Quarters he is answerable that the Instruments, &c., belonging to the Trumpeters are properly packed, loaded, and safely deposited in the New Quarters.'

Musician Edwin McDonnell of the 2nd Life Guards was shot in Bloomsbury on 24 September, 1867, by an Irish Fenian. He died about ten days later and his funeral at Windsor on 7 October was attended by all three Household Cavalry bands, a firing party and bearer party from his Regiment, and, although optional, nearly all of his Regiment who were not on duty in barracks.

In 1863 Charles Cousins of the Second Regiment was appointed Bandmaster of the 2nd Dragoon Guards and in 1874 became Director of

W. J. Cubis, Trumpet Major Second Life Guards 1857–1871

G. J. Rawlins, Trumpet Major Second Life Guards 1874–1879

# TOWN HALL, ELGIN.

Under the Patronage of Colonel Johnston and the Officers, Non-Commissioned Officers, and Men of the 3rd Volunteer Battalion Seaforth Highlanders.

# Two Grand Military Concerts

## FRIDAY, the 25th SEPTEMBER, 1896,

### By the BAND of HER MAJESTY'S

# FIRST LIFE GUARDS

BY KIND PERMISSION OF LIEUT.-COL. S. M. LOCKHART, BART.

Conductor  -  -  -  -  **Mr. Joel Englefield**

Vocalist  -  -  -  **Madame Jessie Strathearn**
*Prima Donna Covent Garden Promenade Concerts, &c.*

Society Artist  -  -  **Mr. Dudley Causton**
*In his Society Musical Sketches as given by him before T.R.H. The Prince and Princess of Wales, &c.*

**MORNING CONCERT**—Doors open at 2·0, commence at 2·30 ; Carriages at 5·0.

**EVENING CONCERT**—Doors open at 7·30, commence at 8 ; Carriages at 10·30.  Early Doors to avoid crush, for Ticketholders only, at 7·15

## SPECIAL RAILWAY ARRANGEMENTS.

The Afternoon Concert has been specially arranged for the convenience of Parties from the Country, and both the Great North of Scotland and Highland Railway Companies have agreed to give Special Cheap Tickets, available to return the same or following day, as under—

THE HIGHLAND RAILWAY- Return Tickets will be issued to Elgin from Keith, Fochabers Town, Hopeman, Inverness, Kingussie, and Intermediate Stations, at a SINGLE FARE and a THIRD (except the following Stations, the Fares from which will be as follow, viz.:—Keith, First Class 2s 3d, Third Class 1s 6d ; Garmouth, First Class 1s 6d. Third Class 9d ; Foot of Garten, First Class 2s 6d, Third Class 3s 10d) by all Trains up to 3 o'clock., available for return on day of issue or following day.

GREAT NORTH OF SCOTLAND RAILWAY—Excursion Tickets will be issued to Elgin from Boat of Garten by the 10·10 A.M. Train ; from Banff by the 11·35 P.M. ; and from Keith by the 1·0 P.M. Train ; also by the 2·0 P.M. Train from Lossiemouth.  Tickets will be valid to return the same or following day by any Ordinary Train.

**Reserved Seats, 3s ; Second Seats and Gallery, 2s ; Back Area, 1s.**

Plan of Hall and Tickets now Ready at JAMES D. YEADON'S, Bookseller, 62 High St., ELGIN.

☞ SEATS CAN BE BOOKED BY POST OR TELEGRAM.

Lithography Printed at "Courant", Elgin.

Music at Kneller Hall where he stayed until 1890. The Cousins Memorial Prize in his honour is still awarded at Kneller Hall.

The First Life Guards, until 1865, had among its instruments the last specimen in a regular army band of a serpent. The size of the Household Cavalry bands gradually increased in number and by the 1870's each had a strength of about thirty-two players.

The bands were still attending summer camp with their Regiments, and during the camps were very much part of the Regiment. With the railways spreading to all points of the compass, the bands began travelling further afield, playing to large appreciative audiences and the Bandmasters in particular were becoming very well known to the civilian population.

Over the years the status within the Regiments of the Bandmaster had risen, and by 1881 as a Warrant Officer he was first of the non-commissioned ranks, after the Regimental Corporal Major. The daily rate of pay of the various ranks shows the Bandmaster to be much better off than the next rank and only fourpence a day below the R.C.M.

| | |
|---|---|
| Regimental Corporal Major | 5/10d per day |
| Bandmaster | 5/6d |
| Quartermaster Corporal | 4/2d |
| Corporal Trumpeter (T/M) | 3/2d |
| Corporal of Horse | 3/- |

From 1882 to 1884 the two Regiments were involved in wars in Egypt and the Soudan. During the 1882 Egyptian Campaign the First Life Guards Trumpeters were Isaac Golding and William Irwin and those of the Second Life Guards Trumpeter Corporal Clarke and Trumpeter John J Barrett. Trumpeter Henry Smith of the first Regiment and Trumpeter Arthur Keightley of the Seconds were part of the Life Guards detachments forming the Heavy Camel Regiment in the Soudan in 1884. Barrett, Golding and Keightley all subsequently became Trumpet Major of their Regiment.

William Van Den Huevel, a Dutchman, took over the band of the First Regiment in 1878 in succession to Waterson and when, in 1887, a German, Carli Zoeller, led the Seconds, both Regiments had a foreign Bandmaster for the first time since 1832. This situation only lasted two years until the unfortunate Zoeller died some days after an accident at the Military Tournament in the Agricultural Hall, Islington, in which the Second Life Guards Band was performing. Both of these Bandmasters had previously led the 7th Hussars Band, Zoeller succeeding Van Den Huevel. Zoeller's

Band of Second Life Guards c.1876

replacement was Leonard Barker from The Greys. In 1890 Joel Englefield of the 18th Hussars replaced Van Den Huevel and five years later Charles Hall, Bandmaster of the Royal Dragoons, succeeded Barker in an association with the Life Guards which was to last until his death in 1922.

The strength of the First's band in 1895 was thirty-six and every man was required to display his skills to the utmost effect, with long tours now commonplace. Having completed a nine-week season at the Crystal Palace they then toured England and Scotland in October and were back north again a month later visiting Newcastle and Glasgow. The following year they played in, among other venues, the Town Hall at Elgin, giving two Grand Military Concerts under the patronage of the Colonel, Officers

State Trumpeters of The Life Guards, Guards Chapel 1966. CPL G. Harris,
MUS S. J. Eden, CPL D. W. Dodson, CPL R. A. Walthew, T/M E. G. Madden,
MUS M. Rose, MUS R. J. Fletcher, MUS W. Marsden, MUS M. Lucas

Band of The Life Guards, Windsor 1971

*Rear Row*    MUS Moore, MUS Hearne, MUS Mean, MUS Graham,
MUS Harman, MUS Morris, MUS Robinson, MUS Dean,
MUS Edward, LCPL Halstead, MUS Rendell, LCPL Taylor,
MUS Webb, MUS Whitworth

*Centre Row*    MUS Nichols, LCPL Jolley, MUS Cooper, LCPL Legge,
LCPL Rose, LCPL Fletcher, MUS Barnes, LCPL Davies,
LCPL Eden, LCPL Lucas, LCPL McQueen, LCPL Wood,
MUS Orchard, MUS Poland, MUS Slater

*Front Row*    LCoH Frost, CoH Henslet, SQMC Taylor,
Capt R. J. Morrisey-Paine (Ajt The Life Guards),
T/M Dodson, Capt A. J. Richards (*Director of Music*),
Colonel I. Baillie (*Regimental Lieutenant-Colonel*),
Lieutenant-Colonel H. D. A. Langley, MBE (*Commanding Officer
The Life Guards*), BCM Dunsmore, Major J. G. Hamilton-Russell
(*Regimental Adjutant*), RCM J. L. Morris, LCoH Marsden,
CPL Hocking, CPL Walthew

*Kettledrummer Second Life Guards c.1830* by J. F. Taylor

*The Drum Horse First Life Guards* by Sir Alfred Munnings. Kettledrummer G. Carter on Paddy II

and Men of the 3rd Volunteer Battalion, Seaforth Highlanders. Singing with the band was Madame Jessie Strathearn 'Prima Donna Covent Garden Promenade concerts etc.' The afternoon programme was:-

| | | |
|---|---|---|
| *Overture* | 'Zampa' | Herold |
| *Piccolo Solo* | 'Pantomimique'<br>Musician Sheppard | Green |
| *Song* | 'The Love for Me'<br>Madame Strathearn | R. Boughton |
| *Ballet Music from* | 'Le Prophete' | Meyerbeer |
| *Cornet Solo* | 'Les Folies'<br>Musician Fenwick | Waldteufel |
| *Original Musical Sketch* | Mr Dudley Causton | |
| *Air Varie* | 'Souvenir des Alpes'<br>1. Cornet: Musician Fenwick<br>2. Eb Clarinet: Corporal Carter<br>3. Bassoon: Musician Francis<br>4. Bb Clarinet: Corporal Hopkins<br>5. Euphonium: Musician Bannister<br>6. Piccolo: Musician Sheppard | Hartmann |
| *Song* | 'The Holy City'<br>Madame Strathearn | Adams |
| *Reminiscences of Wagner* | | Godfrey |
| *Coronation March* | 'Le Prophete' | Meyerbeer |

An interesting item in the evening programme gives an insight into the skill of the performers.

Humorous Variations on a German Air in the respective styles of the
Great Masters                                                    Ochs
Synopsis:- the humour of this piece consists in the rendering of the Variations on one of the simplest of old German airs in such a manner that the style for which each great composer is celebrated is repro-duced in a quaint parody within the limits of a few bars. A short description of the leading idea may be acceptable:-

Theme:- Old Song *'Kommt a Vogel geflogen'*
Variations in the style of 1. Bach – Varying the simple air with learned counterpoint, closing it with an organ fugue. 2. Haydn – A Strong Quartet. 3. Mozart – A Clarinet Solo. 4. Strauss – A Waltz. 5. Verdi – An 'Aria di Bravuro' in the operatic style, with the oft repeated finale of Italian dramatic music. 6. Gounod – Parody on the Garden Scene from 'Faust'. 7. Wagner – Parody on two motives from 'Lohengrin' and 'Tannhauser'. 8. Beethoven – A Violin Sonata. 9. Mendelssohn – (for three instruments) Imitation of the Intermezzo from 'A Midsummer Night's Dream'. 10. Brahms – Parody on Hungarian Dances. 11. Meyerbeer – Here the air is treated in the Grand Heroic style. After an introduction by the drums, the grand scene, 'The Blessing of the Daggers', in 'The Huguenots', is parodied. 12. A Military March.

It is interesting to note that string players played within the military band for this and doubtless other arrangements.

J. J. Barrett, Trumpet Major Second Life Guards 1885–1893, carrying bugle in State Dress

Late in 1897 the Band of the First Life Guards received a handsome present from the 8th Hussars Band, the latter having sent them a very fine St Bernard dog. The reason for the gift or what became of it is unknown.

Corporal of Horse C. Gregory of the Firsts was appointed Bandmaster of the 2nd Battalion Connaught Rangers in 1899, and on 3 May of that year the annual change of station took place, the Firsts moving to Windsor and the Seconds taking their place at Regents Park, while The Blues continued at Knightsbridge. The Regiments remained in these stations for two years instead of the usual one, due to a combination of commitments to the Boer War and celebrations for the new century. After reveille had sounded at midnight, the Band of the Second Life Guards rode out of Regents Park Barracks on 4 December at 1.30 am, playing such tunes as 'The Girl I Left Behind Me', 'The Absent Minded Beggar' and 'Tommy Atkins', as it led its Regiment's Service Squadron through the dark London streets to Waterloo Station where the Squadron entrained for the first part of their journey to South Africa and the Boer War which was to be an experience much different from that of their comrades, who remained in London able to celebrate the dawn of the twentieth century.

Band of First Life Guards c.1900

# CHAPTER 3

# Into the Twentieth Century

At the beginning of the twentieth century Great Britain was heavily committed in the Boer War, and, like most regiments, the Life Guards saw their share of fighting. Both Regiments of Life Guards and the Royal Horse Guards (The Blues) sent a service squadron to form the Household Cavalry Composite Regiment. Over the period of the war each band supplied three men to their service squadron. The First Life Guards trio were Trumpeters E.R. Chase and W. Garrard and Musician J.E. Chillman, and the Second Life Guards Trumpeters R. Griffin and W. Oliver and Musician W.G. Barrow.

Three months into the new century the First Life Guards Band travelled to Dublin for the Royal visit of Queen Victoria during April. On their return to Windsor they were put on stable duty to help cope with the extra remount horses needed for South Africa.

Lance-Corporal J.H. Amers, Second Life Guards, having been the first of his regiment to attend a Bandmasters course at Kneller Hall, was appointed Bandmaster of the 2nd Battalion Devonshire Regiment in June, 1901. Bandmaster Amers later became Flight Lieutenant Amers, MBE, first Director of Music RAF Central Band. Corporal of Horse E Carter, First Regiment, was sent to Morocco in 1902 as an instructor to the Sultan's Band. At the end of 1903 Bandmaster Joel Engelfield of the First Regiment retired and was succeeded by Bandmaster Frederick Haines.

In 1903 the appointment of Trumpeter in Ordinary to the King was abolished. It is from this time that the trumpeters of the Household Cavalry were required to act as State Trumpeters when requested by the Sovereign through the Lord Chamberlain's office. On these occasions State Dress would be worn. If on other occasions State Dress is worn the title of State Trumpeter is not applicable.

The Second Life Guards were by 1906 regularly turning out a string

Trumpeter Pridmore, Second Life Guards c.1903

orchestra, usually under the direction of Corporal Graves. There are many instances of both Life Guards Bands being conducted by Corporals and sometimes Musicians, usually at Regimental functions. 1906 saw the return to his band of Corporal Sheppard, whose return was reported in the *Household Brigade Magazine*:- 'Corporal Sheppard (band) who, for several years past, has been Bandmaster to the West African Field Force, rejoined the 1st Life Guards on the 30th ult. While on the West coast he was awarded an active service medal with two clasps, and in addition, is in possession of the medal for Long Service and Good Conduct, while his methods of teaching the Wild black man Tame music have been reported as unique but most efficacious.'

The Band of the Second Life Guards under the direction of Bandmaster, now 2nd Lieutenant, Hall was the first Household Cavalry band to undertake a major tour abroad when, on 16 August, 1906, Lieutenant Hall and thirty-four musicians set sail in the SS *Canada* bound for Quebec. The band's base during their short stay in Quebec was the Edward VII Hotel. After a concert in the city the next stop was Montreal to play two concerts and then on to Ottawa. The main engagement of the tour was two weeks at the Canadian National Exhibition in Toronto, where their performances were highly acclaimed. While in Toronto the band had many social occasions, a visit to Niagara Falls being the highlight

State Trumpeters Second Life Guards, T/M S. J. Goodhall
Right Hand Man c.1908

Second Life Guards at Combermere c.1911

First Life Guards passing Windsor Police Station c.1912

of the tourist variety. Among many receptions was one given by the combined bands of the Canadian Dragoons, 3rd Royal Grenadiers and the Queen's Own Rifles at which many distinguished persons were present. At the end of the tour Lieutenant Hall was presented with a handsome gold watch. The Band set sail for England aboard the SS *Ottawa* on 8 September and reached Liverpool on 16 September.

After being commissioned, Bandmaster Hall was a rather infrequent visitor to the band, only being present on important parades and engagements, the Band Corporal of Horse conducting on numerous smaller engagements and church services.

In 1907 Bandmaster George Miller began his long association with the First Life Guards and immediately set about the task of forming a first-class string orchestra within the band.

The Second Life Guards in 1908 held many fund-raising events for the new King Edward VII Hospital at Windsor. The Band's contribution was a series of concerts, the funds from which paid to equip two operating rooms.

The military musicians' desire to keep away from all things military, including things with four legs and long faces, is shown in some 'Booby Orders' posted in the NCOs' mess of one of the Household Cavalry regiments in 1909 and also fairly accurately shows the troops' view of the bands:-

'No. 1. It is agreeable to place on record the manner in which the Gentlemen of the Band conducted themselves during their extended stay on the plain. The duties they were called upon to perform were often long and arduous, but on no single occasion were they found wanting (at meal times). The manner in which they took cover in their tents, and remained there until late in the day, was a revelation to anyone not acquainted with a Household Cavalry Band. All fully appreciate the difficult and trying work which falls on the Corporal of Horse Trumpeter at these times, and the fact that the Band were prevented from playing "There's No Place Like Home", instead of the National Anthem, reflects great credit on him and, to some extent, explains the shortage of Scotch and Dry in camp at the present time. The action, however, of some of the musicians in approaching too near the horses is to be deprecated. It should be distinctly understood that this danger is reserved entirely for soldiers. It has been stated that one especially daring Corporal was seen to stroke a black horse; on no account must this occur again. The splendid

Second Life Guards Band c.1913

example set by the Trumpet Major and the Band Corporal of Horse in keeping well clear of these animals was most noticeable and is to be commended. At the same time the Band are to be congratulated on their great improvement in riding since last year, the smart manner in which they mounted and rode out of camp (per G.S.Wagon) this morning was generally commented upon.'

The most important Regimental event of 1913 was the review of the Household Cavalry by the Colonel-in-Chief, His Majesty King George V, which took place at Windsor on 16 June. The bands of both Regiments, together with the Band of the Royal Horse Guards (The Blues), were on parade mounted and massed in the centre of the parade ground. A good description of the Household Cavalry in a book review in *The Spectator* four years earlier fitted this brilliant occasion perfectly: 'Their musicians are a dream in velvet and gold.'

With the exception of the abolition, at the outbreak of the Second World War, of the weekly Sunday Church Parade, the basic working hours of the Bands have changed little over the years: 9.30am to 12.30am and then home, with the band at Windsor charging up Peascod Street to catch the 1.07 train to London. Fifty years later, in 1965, The Life Guards Band were still running up Peascod Street for the 1.07.

Just prior to the First World War a band boy's pay was 2/6d a week. If he could get an appointment as Trumpeter and do duty as a Squadron Officer's trumpeter his pay would jump to 11/6d, which was a man's pay plus twopence a day for the appointment. Presumably the newly appointed Trumpeter would still have to address musicians as Mister. Eight of the Band would be appointed trumpeters, two per squadron. Trumpeters in the Life Guards have for many years been known in the Regiment as 'Fiddlers' and in the 2nd Life Guards musicians were called 'Wind-Jammers'. An amusing incident concerning a squadron trumpeter on a scheme is recalled by Hector Sutherland, formerly Second Life Guards.

Trumpeter Sutherland was squadron trumpeter. Having sounded the Charge, he set off with the whole squadron at a furious gallop for an objective a couple of miles away. On reaching the objective without coming down, Sutherland saw that many had. Men were limping and horses were galloping off in all directions. An officer, Lieutenant Usher, suddenly had an idea. He felt sure that if the trumpeter trotted in the directions of the four points of the compass and blew 'Feed' all the horses would come galloping happily back again. Now this is not such a silly idea when it is realized that, every time the call 'Feed' is sounded in barracks, the horses demonstrate loudly until they get it. So off Trumpeter Sutherland went and blew 'Feed' N.S.E.W. and the horses, instead of coming to the trumpet, galloped off in the opposite direction back to camp where they knew the feed was, leaving many stranded troopers.

The Regiments, complete with trumpeters, were soon to be putting their schemes and training to the test in the horrors which were about to be unleashed throughout Europe.

First Life Guards playing for Grooming, Knightsbridge 1914

# CHAPTER 4

# The Great War

At the outbreak of the Great War the First Life Guards were at Knightsbridge and the Second Life Guards at Windsor. Both Regiments were sent to France in 1914 and, as usual, each took its quota of Trumpeters. Those of the First Regiment were G. Allen, S. Browne, W. Clarke, A. Gaston, R. Godwin, H. Moore, S. Smith and D. Taylor. The Trumpeters on the first draft of the Seconds were T.V. Chinnery and L.T.C. Clifford, followed by W.C. Barnes.

Musician Sidney Browne of the Firsts was killed in action on 20 November, 1914, and Trumpeter H. Moore was wounded. Trumpeter R. Godwin and Musician S. Smith, also of the First Regiment, were both killed while serving in the Guards Machine Gun Regiment.

On 10 February, 1917, the Band of the first Life Guards arrived in France, much to the relief of their Regiment who, for some weeks past, had to endure the strains of a band formed firstly from D Squadron, with mouth organs, concertinas and drums provided by Captain J. J. Astor, and then augmented by players recruited from the other squadrons and formed into a service military band conducted by an officer's servant.

It was once said by an officer of the Life Guards that 'Soldiering would be alright if it only consisted of the band and the mess: no bloody men or horses'. The Regimental Band under Bandmaster George Miller, having been enthusiastically welcomed, played to many regiments and in the many hospitals at Etaples. On one occasion in February or March they paraded, augmented by the men of the service band, as a mounted band, to lead the Regiment on a route march. Sir George Arthur of the Second Life Guards remarked, 'Never, surely, had the band of a Cavalry Regiment been mounted on such a motley collection of cattle'. The Band of the First Regiment returned to England on 27 March, 1917.

At the time when the First Life Guards Band were doing their bit

Second Life Guards Last Parade before going to the Front,
Windsor 9th August 1914

towards the war effort, five young musicians of the Second Life Guards
were auditioning for places at Trinity College of Music. Five scholarships
had been offered to suitable applicants and Corporal Urwin, solo horn of
the Second Life Guards, who was well known to the authorities at Trinity,
had recommended the five young Life Guards. All five were accepted and
one, Hector Sutherland, had the thrill of having as his professor the great
trumpeter Jack Solomon. Unfortunately for the five Trinity College
students not much time was available for practice, with reinforcements
being sent continually to the Regiment in France and the band being
called upon to groom from three to six horses each a day.

In July, 1918, it was the turn of the Second Life Guards Band to visit
France. The Band duly paraded at Combermere Barracks feeling like
fighting soldiers as only bandsmen can after having done anything
remotely soldierlike; the action that prompted this feeling was having
removed the wire stiffening from their service dress caps. After marching

through cheering crowds to Windsor Station and arriving at Folkestone, the Band stayed overnight and paraded at 7 a.m. the next day ready to board ship for France, only to be ordered immediately back to Windsor. On arriving at Windsor, Major Hall, the Director of Music, decided, after the triumphal send-off the day before, to return to barracks by a backstreet route. All went well until a local youngster spotted the Band and shouted some uncomplimentary remarks which prompted several others to join in the jeering.

Ten days later they departed from Windsor in a much-subdued manner and finally left Folkestone en route for France. After landing at Boulogne on 4 August the Band marched to St Martins camp which was a clearance depot for all battle fronts. The next day they marched back to Boulogne station where two clean cattle trucks had been reserved for a journey north, destination unknown, which was the same wherever they were going. Some of the journeys were so slow that men would jump off the train as it entered a village, buy some milk and fruit and jump back on. Their destination on the first journey turned out to be Flesselle and the welcome sight of shoulder flashes reading '2nd Life Guards M.G.Gds', the Regiment having been converted into the 2nd Battalion Guards

First Life Guards at Knightsbridge 1915

Machine Gun Regiment. After some hurried refreshment a concert was given to a large and appreciative audience. One slight set-back was the non-appearance of the side drum stand, drum sticks, triangle and box of tricks. The drummer, Musician Grace, had seen them unloaded at Boulogne and knew they must be about somewhere. A motorcycle and sidecar was immediately dispatched to Boulogne. The concert began without a side drum but someone soon produced a pair of sticks with knobs on and a chair made an improvised drum stand. The Band were considered very fortunate in their accommodation which was a spacious barn with plenty of clean straw. Luck was on their side. The roof had many gaping holes but the weather was fine. The next day the Regimental armourer made a serviceable drum stand and a triangle, which was a necessity as the original kit chased the Band all over France.

One very sad duty the band performed in France was for the funeral service of Lieutenant V.J. Ferguson of the Regiment.

An appreciative Royal Flying Corps station actually sent thirty-six men on leave on the day of a Second Life Guards Band concert in order to give the band double rations. Another memorable day was spent entertaining Canadian nurses at the Headquarters, near Arras, of General Curry, after which the band were treated to steak and kidney pie cooked by the General's chef.

Four years after the war Lieut-General Sir Alexander Godley, KCB, KCMG, wrote in the *Household Brigade Magazine*:-

'In September, 1918, during the second Battle of the Somme, I was commanding the 3rd Corps and was fortunate enough to have in it the 2nd Life Guards Machine Gun Battalion, and to have the Band of the 2nd Life Guards placed at my disposal. It was, of course, the greatest treat to us all to hear such a band in the Somme desert, and I was very anxious that as many of the troops as possible should share it. Accordingly, one day I asked Col. Stanley to let the Band play at an advanced Brigade Headquarters, arranged for as many men of the Battalions as possible to hear it and took the opportunity of going myself to combine paying a visit to the Brigade with forming one of the audience.

'The Headquarters was situated at the bottom of a wide, open valley in very open country. When I came in view of it, from about a mile away, instead of a large and expectant crowd, the only sign of life that I could see was the Band marching to, and nearing, the rendezvous. The reason was not far to seek. The Huns were shelling

33

MUS Jones, Solo Cornet First Life Guards

CoH H. J. Harman, Solo Cornet Second Life Guards

the head of the valley, and to those perhaps more intimately acquainted with their habits than the band of this distinguished regiment, it was obvious that their attentions would soon reach the foot of it. But, nothing daunted by the absence of audience or the approach of shelling, Major Hall and his gallant men marched on. They had made their engagement and they meant to fulfil it. They arrived and began to play. The Brigadier and a few of the bolder spirits of the headquarters in amazement put their heads out of their dug-outs and, as far as they could hear for the noise of bursting shells, were rewarded by a musical discourse of a quality such as I suppose, no one ever heard in anything approaching such a situation. But shells were now bursting all round and close to this devoted band, so slowly, reluctantly, and with befitting dignity they moved some few hundred years further back and got to work again, and I noticed, from my comparatively distant point of vantage, that whatever small audience there had been before, so far from following them, had once more gone to ground. again the shelling pursued the band and again it beat a dignified retreat, but it had come to play and play it would, shelling or no shelling, audience or no audience, and after a few more exchanges of this kind with the Huns, persistence prevailed and the programme was triumphantly concluded.

'My feelings at the prospect of having to account to Colonel Stanley for the mangled remains of his precious band can be better imagined than described, but fortunately there were no casualties, and never, I am sure, in the history of war, did any band get a fiercer shelling or stand firm better than did the Band of His Majesty's 2nd Life Guards on this occasion.'

The next place was Querrio and playing for an inspection of the 22nd London Regiment by HM King George V. Three days later members of the Band were wandering through Troans Wood which was littered with dead Germans and many dead of those same gallant 22nd Londons. In between Querrio and Troans Wood, Bray and Mericourt had been visited. The last billets of the Band in the battlefields for the time being were a deserted German dug-out headquarters.

Shortly after, the Band was ordered to Paris for the celebrations of the anniversary of the Battle of the Marne. This took place in the Trocadero (later rebuilt as the Palais de Chaillot) with the President of France, many important statesmen and all the army commanders not at the front present. After four days of luxury in the Grand Palais on the Champs Elysées, the next move was to a rat-infested bunker at Houdain on the Lens front. Eventually on 1 October, 1918, the Second Life Guards Band sailed from Boulogne for England. Among their company were five worried young musicians hoping that Trinity College of Music had not cancelled their scholarships. Also aboard was the much-travelled drum kit which rejoined the Band just as the ship was about to sail.

On arrival at Windsor the Band mess was abolished and the musicians given the same duties to perform as troopers, which meant grooming and exercising the horses, who had been kept up to full regimental strength, even while the main body of the Regiment was abroad. With more and more men being recruited, a contingent arrived from Trinidad, most of whom joined the Second Life Guards. One, Oswald Smith, who was only fourteen years old, was put into the Band and became an excellent trumpeter.

The war ended on 11 November, 1918, and that same evening the Second Life Guards Band, with torch-bearers from the Windsor Fire Brigade, assembled at the barrack gate and led cheering crowds of Windsorians through the crowded streets to Eton College, there to be joined by the college boys who, with the Windsor people, made a choir of over a thousand voices.

In March, 1919, all the Guards Regiments marched past His Majesty King George V led by the two regiments of Life Guards with their bands. At Westminster Abbey, on 2 April, a Household Cavalry Requiem was attended by the Royal Family and a huge congregation. The three Household Cavalry Bands, massed, played Massenet's Angelus and the Eton Memorial March. Sir Arthur Sullivan's anthem 'Though I walk through the Valley of the Shadow of Death' was, like the other pieces, appropriate for the occasion. It was appropriate also that the Life Guards should perform Sir Arthur's music, as shortly before his death he had visited one of the bands and thanked the Gentlemen of the Life Guards for the way they rendered his compositions.

Boy Oswald Smith, Second Life
Guards, 1918

# CHAPTER 5

# The Amalgamation and After

At the end of the 'War to end Wars' in 1919 the Army was subjected to reductions in all arms of the Service by the 'Geddes Axe' named after its sponsor.

The two Regiments of Life Guards were not to escape the axe and were amalgamated in July, 1922, when two squadrons of the Second Life Guards rode into Regents Park Barracks to join with two squadrons of the First Regiment. The band of the new regiment, The Life Guards (1st and 2nd), was under the direction of Lieutenant Henry Eldridge, formerly First Life Guards. Major Hall of the Seconds, although expected to retire on the amalgamation, was directed by the Army Council to remain on the active list until he attained the age of sixty-five. Unfortunately he died in October, 1922, barely five weeks after conducting the Band for the last time at the Central Hall, Westminster, on 11 September.

The squadrons retained their former regimental dress, i.e. A and B Squadrons as First Life Guards, C and D Squadrons as Second Life Guards. The Band and Trumpeters probably kept their own regimental uniforms, the difference being so small as to be almost unnoticeable. The one exception was the blue crossbelt cord of the Seconds which was changed to the red of the Firsts.

The manner of tying the cords on the cavalry duty trumpet of the amalgamated regiment follows the custom of the First Regiment. On the bell end the cords are tied round the lower tubing while at the mouthpiece end they are round the tubing into which the mouthpiece fits. The Second Regiment additionally wound the cord round the bell before tying to the bell end. The method as described for the First Regiment was also at one time used on the state trumpets of both Regiments. At the present time they are simply looped round the tubing either side of the banner.

Hector Sutherland, formerly of the Second Life Guards Band, wrote in his book *They Blow Their Own Trumpets*:

Band of Second Life Guards, Royal Tournament, Olympia 1921

*Back Row*   MUS A. Woodford, MUS Look, MUS Elston, MUS K. Woodford, CPL Barnes, CPL Pipe

*Third Row*   MUS Reardon, MUS Tutt, MUS Keenan, MUS Hazel, MUS Silwood, CPL White, CPL Norton, MUS Whitehead, MUS Jackson

*Second Row*  MUS Childs, MUS Chinnery, MUS Sargeant, MUS Langston, MUS Collier, MUS Grace, CPL Bullock, MUS Clifford, CPL Thompson, MUS McCarthy, CPL French

*Front Row*   MUS Morris, CoH Harman, Maj Hall, T/M Warren, MUS Titman, MUS Crisp

Band of The Life Guards (1st and 2nd) c.1923

'All went on with apparent smoothness and terribly smart turnout, each regiment jealously proud of its own customs and traditions, neither one giving way to the other, which in many ways seemed to make for greater efficiency. Far too efficient as far as the Band was concerned, for instead of rolling in casually about 10 a.m. our men of the Second Life Guards had to actually parade for inspection at 9.30 a.m. and were ticked off right and left if a boot wasn't sufficiently highly polished or a spur lacked the gleam of the burnisher. Then at 10 a.m. sharp the new Musical Director would take the Band at practice with the non-stop don't-waste-a-minute zeal of the conscientious fanatic. I found myself still very much at the end of the cornet section, with our solo cornet Corporal of Horse Harman having to take a back seat, along with our other soloists, to the musicians of the First Life Guards. It was an unavoidable yet most difficult situation, for had Major Hall continued in the new Regiment the soloists would naturally have been from the Second Life Guards, in which case the First Life Guards would have felt the same sense of frustration which descended upon our men.'

Several former Second Life Guards musicians, not liking the First Regiment's discipline and bull, now the order in the Life Guards (1st & 2nd), found a variety of ways of getting a discharge. One rather drastic way out was taken by Musician Crisp who transferred to the Royal Horse Guards (The Blues). The strength of the Band at this time was about thirty-seven: one Director of Music, one Corporal of Horse, one Corporal, six Lance-Corporals, twenty-five Musicians and Trumpeters and three Boys.

Life in the new band soon settled into a routine with C.A. Bryant, formerly First Regiment, as Trumpet Major and Corporal of Horse Harry Harman of the Second Life Guards as Band Corporal of Horse. In June, 1923, Trumpet Major Bryant retired and Corporal of Horse Harman was appointed Trumpet Major, which position he held until December, 1930.

Gramophone recording continued under Eldridge almost as frequently as under Miller. In September, 1926, Lieutenant Eldridge died suddenly at Regents Park Barracks and the Band were without a director until 12 October when Mr W.J. Gibson of the Royal Tank Corps was appointed. The Band under Lieutenant Gibson were still almost living in recording studios but did find time for some other engagements.

Possibly the most important Regimental event of the late twenties was the presentation of new Standards to the Regiment by His Majesty King George V on 24 June, 1927, on Horseguards Parade, when the Band performed mounted, massed with The Blues. Most of the Band horses on this parade were greys, some having been borrowed from the Royal Dragoons stationed at Hounslow.

The amalgamation was finally completed in June, 1928, when (1st & 2nd) was dropped from the Regiment's name and it became The Life Guards. Changes in uniform are fully explained in Chapter 15. One other significant event in 1928 was the first broadcast by The Life Guards Band on 21 September at 7.45 p.m. The programme was:-

A POPULAR CONCERT
Arranged by ALLAN BROWN, F.R.C.O.
THE BAND OF THE LIFE GUARDS
(By permission of Lieut.-Col. The Hon. G.V.A.
MONCKTON-ARUNDELL, D.S.O., O.B.E.)
Conducted by Lieut. W.J. GIBSON
Relayed from the Kingsway Hall

BAND and GRAND ORGAN
Overture to 'Ruy Blas'                    *Mendelssohn*

GARDA HALL (Soprano) and Orchestra
Charmant oiseau (Charming bird, from The
    'Pearl of Brazil')                    *F. David*
    Solo Flute : Musician G. McBRIDE

BAND
Selection from 'The Show Boat'            *Kern*

ROBERT PITT and LANGTON MARKS
Calling the British Smiles
ALLAN BROWN (Grand Organ)
Finale from Organ Symphony No. 1 in D Minor
    (Op. 42)                             *Guilmant*

HELENA MILLAIS (Entertainer)
BAND and GRAND ORGAN
March of the Knights of the Grail ('Parsifal') *Wagner*

Having reached all corners of the country on the airwaves in 1928, the following September the Band travelled about as far as was possible in Britain when they visited Aberdeen for a fortnight of concerts. They did, according to newspaper reports, make a great impression, which was borne out when they attracted a record attendance at the final Saturday concert at Hazlehead.

The high standards set by the Band over the years is verified by the impact many former members made in the civilian musical profession, playing in the leading symphony and theatre orchestras of the day.

When the Empire Theatre, Leicester Square, was at the height of its fame the whole of the brass section were ex-members or members of the Life Guards, and later the brass of Daly's Theatre was also composed totally of Life Guards. The musicians were certainly helped by Regimental Standing Orders, one paragraph saying:- 'Leave may be granted to the Band on the Monday of each week to enable attendance at rehearsals for private engagements.'

In October, 1931, Lieutenant Gibson retired and Lieutenant S.S. Smith appointed from the Royal Dragoons. Unfortunately for the Band the new Director had a deserved reputation as a master horseman and champion pistol shot and after a couple of years most of his time was spent pursuing these interests to the detriment of the Band. He would be out some mornings hunting or just riding and at other times at shooting practice. Although under Lieutenant Smith the classification the Band attained from Kneller Hall inspections improved from 'Fair' in 1932 to 'Very Good' in 1937/8, some sections of the Band had sunk to a very low standard and the strength had decreased from thirty-five in 1931 to twenty-nine in 1938. Lieutenant Smith left the Regiment on 9 May, 1938, to be replaced by Lieutenant Albert Lemoine from the Royal Tank Corps.

Lieutenant Lemoine, who arrived with a reputation as both a hard man and an excellent musician, lost no time setting about the task of raising the Band to its former stature. One of his first acts was on the retirement of Trumpet Major Woodford, when he arranged for Trumpet Major E.C. (Mick) Leonard of the Royal Scots Greys to be transferred to The Life Guards as Trumpet Major, something quite unheard of as most transfers into Guards bands had usually been sergeants in their former bands but on transfer reverted to the rank of Musician.

As had been the practice over many years, all Musicians and Trumpeters were placed on the trumpet guard roll to do twenty-four hour barrack guard as Duty Trumpeter. Most of the older or more senior Musicians did not do the guards as there was another roll of Band Boys, younger Musicians and Trumpeters who did the guards for payment of 6/- a guard, paid by the older men. A boy's weekly pay was 7/- of which he drew 3/-, 4/- was stopped for damages etc., so an extra guard a week trebled his pay.

Lieutenant Lemoine soon had the Band up to strength, both numerically and musically, and once again the Band were offered prestigious engagements. One of particular note was to record, in 1939, together with the London Symphony Orchestra the music for the film *Victoria the Great*, starring Anna Neagle.

One innovation Lemoine tried was to have a side drummer in the mounted band. He also wanted a mounted cymbal player but the opposition from all quarters won the day. The side drummer, Musician W. Ferris, was used on Trooping the Colour in 1939. For whatever reason, this was the first and last time a mounted side drummer was used in The Life Guards Band.

Rehearsal for Trooping the Colour 1939 with mounted side drummer (right of picture)

# CHAPTER 6

# 1939 – 45

When the Second World War began The Life Guards and the Royal Horse Guards each supplied troops for the Household Cavalry Composite Regiment which left for Palestine on 9 February, 1940, its name was later changed to the First Household Cavalry Regiment. The Band's contribution was five trumpeters:- Trumpet Corporal of Horse F. Forder and Trumpeters F. Andrews, J. Billyeald, T.S.R. Grisenthwaite and W.H. Stevens. The newly formed Household Cavalry Training Regiment was at Windsor and the Household Cavalry Reserve Regiment, to whom the Band was attached, was at Knightsbridge.

After the First Household Cavalry Regiment changed from a mounted unit to a mechanized regiment, Trumpeters Billyeald and Stevens were relieved of their appointments of Trumpeter and reverted to Troopers. While on a wireless instructors course in Cairo Stevens was visited by Grisenthwaite who had, in the meantime, received a commission into the 101st Royal Tank Regiment. Trooper Stevens eventually became Squadron Corporal Major of D Squadron. Corporal of Horse Forder, who had been the colonel's Trumpeter, left the Regiment and joined the Cairo Military Band.

Life in the Band went on much as usual, morning practice, free afternoons, and many of the engagements of pre-war days still on the Band calendar. Broadcasts particularly aimed at the troops increased, as did the bombing.

Captain Lemoine, now with the opportunity of enlisting top civilian musicians, transferred four junior members of the Band to line regiments in order to create vacancies. One of the new intake was Harry Parr Davies who was eventually to compose nineteen musical shows which included *The Lisbon Story*. While still at school Parr Davies had written songs for Gracie Fields and on leaving became her composer and accompanist.

Harry Parr-Davies, Composer Member of the Band during World War II

During his career he wrote many film scores and famous songs. Musician Parr Davies was highly thought of by Captain Lemoine and was given the doubtful privilege of being permitted to smoke during rehearsals.

Neil Sanders, who became one of the outstanding horn players of the post-war period, was another Lemoine acquisition. Musician Sanders' aversion to military life prompted him, on one occasion, to call Lemoine a pig. When asked to repeat what he had said he replied, 'You are a pig Sir,' and was promptly locked up.

The London Symphony Orchestra provided the Band with Jock Ashby, principal trombone, and Dennis MacManson, a violinist who was used as a soloist with the military band performing pieces such as 'Schon Rosmarin' by Kreisler and Gounod's 'Ave Maria'.

The Band remained at Knightsbridge throughout the blitz and had a constant companion in Joey, a mongrel dog, who belonged to Trumpeter Andrews. Joey had the free run of Knightsbridge Barracks and knew all the places where food could be had. Joey's attachment to the Band was well known in the Household Cavalry Reserve Regiment, for he used to sit among the Band when they were on parade, but on the departure of the Reserve Regiment and subsequent replacement by a unit of the Royal

Trumpeters E. G. Madden and B. J. Clarke with Joey

Army Service Corps, the Service Corps Commanding Officer ordered Joey's removal from barracks. Musician E.G. Madden took Joey under his wing and Joey lived the rest of his life in the care of Mrs Madden in Southend. A couple of years after Joey's removal to Southend the Band were engaged to play on Southend bandstand. One of the musicians, Lofty Garbutt, spotted Joey in the crowd and whistled him; like a flash Joey was on the bandstand, much to the delight of all the Band including Captain Lemoine.

In late 1941 the Band moved to Combermere Barracks, Windsor, but still carried out engagements in the London parks and seaside resorts, now wearing the drab khaki battledress. The Speaker of the House of Commons, Captain the Right Hon. E.A. Fitzroy, PC, a former Life Guard officer, died in March, 1943, and four trumpeters of The Life Guards attended his funeral.

Funeral of the Speaker of the House of Commons, TPTRS. J. Tillotson, E. G. Madden, B. J. Clarke, H. B. Dunsmore, March 1943

Clarinet Section St James's Park 1943, CPL L. Hazel, MUSN's D.P. O'Donovan,
W. Johnson, W. G. Hambleton, F. E. Perks

Cornet Section St James's Park 1943, T/M C. J. Leonard, MUS H. B. Dunsmore,
CPL E. D. Mirams, MUSN's W. Hazelwood, B. J. Clarke, N. Bearcroft

Tenor Section St James's Park 1943, Euphonium MUS A. Cawdery,
Bassoon MUS H. E. Sloane, Saxes MUSN's R. F. Kennedy, G. Henley

Basses St James's Park 1943, String Bass MUS E. Ineson, Brass MUSN's G. Williams,
R. McDonald

Trombones, St James's Park 1943.
*Foreground* MUS J. Ashby. *Behind* MUS R. L. B. Garbutt

Drums St James's Park 1943, MUSN's G. Sweetland, E. G. Madden, W. Connor, K/D N. Harris

Captain Lemoine and Band c.1943

On 19 August, 1944, orders came for the Band to go to France. The diary of former Musician Norman Bearcroft, later Lieutenant-Colonel Bearcroft, National Secretary for Bands and Songster Brigades, the Salvation Army, tells us the first step was a move to a camp near Gosport on the 21st. The following day the Band boarded an American tank landing craft, *Ops Neptune*, manned by British seamen. At 9 o'clock the craft was packed with tanks and lorries, the only passengers being The Life Guards Band and the band of the 'Shiny Tenth' Hussars. Six or seven hours later the craft moved a little way off Portsmouth, where it waited for the convoy to assemble by midnight, then moved off round the Isle of Wight.

Landing on Juno Beach, Normandy, at 6.45 pm on 23 August the musicians' first task was to help with the loading of British casualties and wounded German prisoners, while waiting for transport to St Aubin-sur-Mer. The camp at St Aubin was a rest camp for soldiers from the front. One man resting at the time was Corporal of Horse Dennis Meakin of

The Life Guards, later Quartermaster and Lieutenant-Colonel. On 24 August an Irish Guards Sergeant remarked to Corporal of Horse Meakin, 'The Household Cavalry must have suffered heavy casualties'. 'Hardly any, why?' replied Meakin, 'Well a new Household Cavalry draft has just arrived and they are mostly midgets,' said the sergeant. On going outside to view the new draft, Meakin was confronted by Captain Lemoine and the Band of The Life Guards. It should be said here that there were until 1976 no height restrictions for the Band. On Saturday the 26th the Band moved to St Germain de Croit, only to find they were not expected and had to sleep under hedges with only greatcoats for bedding.

The following day instruments were unpacked, oiled and later played in a concert given at Conde for the Guards Armoured Division. On the 28th concerts were played at Galigne and Vassy before moving to Lande Patry. Concerts at Tinchebray on 31 August and St Clare Dehalauze on 1 September followed. The 2nd of September was spent travelling to Fleurs and very rough accommodation in a German barracks. Next day a concert was played in a local cinema and then almost a week with nothing of note before moving to Morgny on 11 September for a concert on the 12th at Notre Dame d'Isle. A day of general cleaning up, change of clothing and a mobile bath made Wednesday 13 September memorable. Three more days of concerts, starting at Etrapagny, then playing for civilians at Limerick and St Pierre d'Autils and in the evening to the Royal Artillery at Bonnières. A brief period of comparative luxury, spent in the Three Merchants Hotel in Les Andelys, started on 20 September. After playing for local civilians, the Band provided the music on the 22nd for a swank (inspection) parade of the Scots Guards, followed by a long journey to give a concert the same evening for the Grenadier Guards. Although in the middle of a world war, time was still found for football and they played at a match between the Grenadiers and the French. The next day was spent entertaining at the local hospital and the following evening playing at a sports meeting.

After the liberation of Brussels, which had been led by a troop of the Second Household Cavalry Regiment, the Band played their part in the celebrations. Leaving Les Andelys on 3 October, they arrived in Brussels to enjoy the Splendid Hotel. Arriving at the hotel in the evening in two brand-new three-ton lorries, they unloaded and settled in. The following morning, all being ready to board the three-tonners, they were nowhere to be seen and, indeed, they were never seen again. A very strong rumour was that they had been sold by two of the Band.

Broadcasting in Brussels 1944

Another story of the time concerned the Trumpet Major who had, during the travels in France, acquired a leather-covered armchair which was his comfort when travelling in the back of three-ton lorries. Once, when the Director of Music was not travelling, it was the Trumpet Major's lot to travel in the cab with the driver. Seizing the opportunity to give vent to their jealousies, the band threw the chair out of the lorry over a bridge and into a river, and the chair, like the new three-tonners, was never seen again.

Two or three days after arriving in the Belgian capital, the Band were in a studio broadcasting.

On Saturday, 7 October, a concert was given outside the Theatre Royal Opera House, Brussels, playing a programme which included Steps of Glory, Orpheus in the Underworld, Charm of the Waltz, The Chocolate Soldier, The Firefly, excerpts from *Aida* and Five Minutes with Cole Porter. Several more performances were given in Brussels before leaving at 12 midnight on 24 October for Holland, where they arrived at 8.30 am. Later that day it was the Welsh Guards' turn to sample the music of The Life Guards on an inspection parade at the Divisional Club. Not to be outdone, the Coldstream Guards held a similar parade the next day at the same venue. During the evening the Band played for their own regiment at the front line; 'rather noisy', reminiscent of the 2nd Life Guards in 1918; next day, another for the Grenadiers. During this short stay in Holland the Band lived under canvas, four or five miles from the front line which was the River Maas.

Saturday, 28 October, back to Brussels, up next morning to take the Royal Corps of Signals to church, and then horse-racing in the afternoon. On or about 4 November the Band, who by now were known as 'Monty's Pets', played for him at a dinner he gave for all the senior officers who had taken part in the Battle of El Alamein. Nothing more of note until a concert on the 8th at Ancien Belgique. The following day rehearsals began for a parade on the 11th at the Palais de Bosarts. The rehearsal finished at two in the morning; this was followed later in the day by another, then a performance that evening. Saturday the 11th was the main show, in the presence of Her Majesty Queen Mary the Queen Mother. On Monday 13 November a concert was given at Renaix. On Tuesday the 14th the Band said goodbye to the people of Brussels and moved to Tessenderloo. There the accommodation was a disused house, very dirty and no beds. Musician Bearcroft took the opportunity of getting away from the squalid place as often as possible by playing the organ in the local church.

On Friday, 17 November they were on the road bound for Ashe, Belgium, with a Corporal Major detailed as navigator, but Captain Lemoine insisted that he was in charge and would therefore navigate. Some hours later the Musicians were asking why all the road and shop signs were in German. When the driver heard the answer, The Life Guards Band tour of Germany came to a very speedy end. The following day they were back in Holland by a more direct route, to live in a theatre in Geleen. Concerts were played every day, with a church parade on Sunday the 19th and then, on the 26th, another move took them to Brunsum. Musician Bearcroft remarked, 'The trip has been so badly organized that they had done only about a quarter of the playing they might have done, and a rumour is about that the Band will sail for home before Christmas.' On arrival in Brunsum they were billeted with civilians, who had no choice in the matter but were only required to provide bare accommodation. The billet of Bearcroft and Corporal Jimmy Buck was a back kitchen with a stone floor. There was nothing to eat and the toilet facilities

53

were down the garden. Six days were spent under these conditions, which also included eating in a café two miles away, playing in a cinema six miles away and having a bath down a coal mine.

On Sunday 3 December they played a concert at Hoensbrock and on the 5th played for the Second Household Cavalry Regiment at Ashe. They played again for the H.C.R. on the 9th at Waterschei and afterwards slept on the floor 'as usual'. More concerts, inspections and prize-givings were undertaken over the next few days. One date easily remembered was 15 December when the dance band played for the U.S. Air Force on the night Glen Miller died. A concert on 19 December was cancelled five minutes before starting time, when the Regiment, as part of the Guards Armoured Division, were ordered up to assist the Americans at the Battle of the Bulge.

Christmas Eve until New Year's Day, 1945, was completely free. A concert in a casino in Belgium started the ball rolling again, then on 8 January they moved to a snowy Eindhoven into civilian digs and concerts were given in the local hospital and theatre. Nijmegen was the next stop, living in a hospital, then a brief period of leave in Brussels, followed, on 10 February, by a return to the Belgian capital.

The eventual return to England was on 9 March and a number of the Band, who had bought new instruments while on the Continent, had to throw their old instruments overboard in order to get through Customs.

# CHAPTER 7

# Peace

At the end of the European War in May, 1945, with celebrations throughout Great Britain and Europe, bands were particularly busy. Eight Trumpeters of The Life Guards went to France soon after peace was declared and the Band returned to France in August to take part in the Victory Parade through Paris. London's Victory Parade on 8 June, 1946, was another long march for the Band. The busiest section of the Band at this time was undoubtedly the dance band, celebration dances being a regular excuse for good times. The dance band at this time was under the direction of saxophonist Corporal R.F. (Ken) Kennedy and continued under him until his retirement in the early sixties. The nucleus of the dance band performed as a civilian combination known as the Kenmon Players, a title taken from the names of Kennedy and the band's pianist Corporal Tony Monaghan.

With the return of the horses to the Household Cavalry, extra accommodation was needed at Combermere Barracks where recruits were being trained, also at Knightsbridge where each Regiment eventually supplied one mounted squadron for State Duties. The mounted squadrons each had on strength three trumpeters.

In September, 1946, in order to gain the extra space, The Life Guards Band, with that of The Blues, was moved to the Etonian Country Club at Clewer, Windsor. The most memorable happening during the Etonian Club period were the Windsor floods of March, 1947. One evening during this month, three Life Guards band boys went to see a film at the Empire Cinema in Peascod Street, Windsor. Afterwards, on the trek back to the Etonian Club, the trio, on reaching Oxford Road, found the only way back to Clewer was to wade through chest-high floodwater. Boy Leslie Downs had in his possession three pound notes which, on a weekly wage of ten shillings, was a small fortune. His one thought was for the safety of his fortune which he placed in his cap and held it firmly in place as he waded back, determined that, come hell or high water, nothing would rob him of his princely sum.

The two bands had their own cookhouse and staff at the Etonian Club but otherwise they were stranded from other services, including the Post, although one service they did have was the telephone, with the younger members having to do duty as switchboard operator. The enterprising youngsters in the Band acquired a punt from the nearby River Thames and would punt along Oxford Road where the local inhabitants would draft letters and give orders for supplies to the musicians who would park their craft at the Goswells, shop in Peascod Street and return, loaded with supplies for themselves and the local residents.

One member of the Band at this time, destined for fame in the musical world, was Musician Colin Davis, later Sir Colin, Music Director of the Royal Opera and of the BBC Symphony Orchestra. In January, 1947, Captain Lemoine received a letter from another famous figure of the music world: the composer Percy Grainger.

'Dear Major Lemoine [sic]

When in England recently I listened with such pleasure and admiration to your broadcasts, relishing the superb musicianship of your renderings and the rich and exquisitely balanced tone of your band.

'Amongst the numbers I particularly enjoyed were
Eric Coates : Summer Days.
Strauss-Korngold : Vienna Woods
Auber : Masaniello

'I have always been in love with the military band as a medium, composing my 'Lads of Wamphrey' March (direct for band) in 1905, when I was in touch with the Coldstream Guards Band. I am taking the liberty of sending you the score of this march, and am asking my London publishers to send you the score of my *Lincolnshire Posy*, also composed direct for bands. Expect you would like to have the band parts for these 2 numbers. I will be happy to send them to you, if you will kindly let me know how many clarinet, cornet (etc.) parts you would like.

I am sending (with the score) a photo of myself, in memory of the great pleasure I had in hearing your glorious broadcasts.
Yours cordially
Percy Grainger'

Victory Parade, Paris August 1945

Cavalry Memorial Sunday c.1947 SQMC G. A. Lawn leading

Barrack Guard, Knightsbridge 1947. Trumpeter R. McDonald

On 10 November, 1947, the Band, with that of The Blues, provided four State Trumpeters and a composite mounted band, all in State Dress, under the direction of Captain Lemoine, for the Lord Mayor's procession. This band was made up of those with pre-war riding experience. The remainder of the Band, who had not passed a pre-war riding course, had to undergo equitation training at Windsor in 1949.

In 1948 State Trumpeters of The Life Guards played their part in the biggest event of the year, the Olympic Games at Wembley, performing at the opening and closing ceremonies under the direction of Trumpet Major Smith. For five months of 1948 the Regiment furnished the Windsor Castle Guard. The Guard was usually led to and from the castle by the Regimental Band, who also provided the Trumpeter of the Guard each day. At the end of that year Windsor Borough Council decided to hold a carol service at the Queen Victoria statue. Major Lemoine and the Band played before and during the service which became an annual event and is still on the Windsor calendar and also that of whichever Household Cavalry Band is in Windsor at the time.

With National Service still in force, Major Lemoine used it to the advantage of the Band. National Servicemen could not normally serve in The Life Guards Band but several students of promise from the London music colleges were given the opportunity of serving in the band instead of doing their National Service in other regiments, during which they would have become fighting soldiers liable to be sent anywhere in the world. Later a three-year period of regular service was introduced and those due for National Service had then to sign on for three years in order to get into the Band, but even now there were one or two exceptions. The authorized establishment at this time was forty-nine, but, in order to enlist these students, who were mainly string players, Major Lemoine took them on strength as troopers and at times the Band was over sixty strong. The advantages of joining The Life Guards Band after completing their General Military Training were postings only to Knightsbridge or Windsor and reporting into barracks on Thursdays only to collect their pay. Any work they were expected to do amounted to the occasional orchestral date at Windsor Castle, Buckingham Palace or Regimental functions. But the greatest advantage was their continued attendance at college and the opportunities of engagements with the major London

One of the last Parades for the Red Plumes, Combermere c.1950

orchestras. On the few occasions these string players wore uniform a regular complaint from them was that the overalls, which had to be crease-free, were held up by army canvas braces and were therefore extremely uncomfortable when playing the violin. Following these complaints, Major Lemoine paraded the string players at Victoria Barracks in scarlet tunics and overalls and then ordered them to touch their toes. The resulting parting of buttons from overalls convinced Major Lemoine of the legitimacy of the complaint and he gave permission for elastic braces to be worn in future.

About 1958 a mini-disaster struck the string players when they were made to learn the cavalry trumpet and were subsequently placed on the trumpet guard roll. One violinist, Dudley Houston, having signed on as a regular, had, in 1951, undergone a Household Cavalry equitation course. One of the first of these several string players was Norman Nelson who was to become principal first violin of the BBC Symphony Orchestra and later Concert Master of the Vancouver Symphony Orchestra. Other positions later held by former members included:- Leader; Royal Liverpool Philharmonic, English National Opera, Scottish Opera, Co-Leader; Royal Philharmonic, The Philharmonia, English Chamber Orchestra, Co-Concert Master; Houston Symphony, Principal Second Violin; London Philharmonic and Royal Philharmonic, Principal Cellist; BBC Symphony and Repetiteur; Royal Opera House.

From June, 1949, until September, 1951, the Band was stationed with various Foot Guard battalions at Victoria Barracks, Windsor. There were many amusing misunderstandings between The Life Guards and Foot Guards, neither one understanding the ways and traditions of the other. There was the occasion, after a young musician had swept rubbish over the side of the stairs on to the Regimental Sergeant Major of the Coldstream Guards, of all the musicians hiding in lockers or blowing the first instrument that came to hand in order to escape the wrath of the RSM. Another brush with Foot Guards occurred in late 1951 when the Band were playing for dinner at Windsor Castle. Two young Life Guard band boys, who had been part of the fatigue party transporting the music stands and instruments, were afterwards walking down towards the Henry VIII gateway when they passed a party of the castle guard in grey greatcoats. The two boys were immediately stopped by a sergeant of the guard who demanded, 'Why had they not saluted the Officer?' Boy R.A. Walthew replied, 'We didn't know he was an officer'. 'Couldn't you see he was carrying a sword?' snapped the sergeant. Walthew's truthful reply, 'Everyone in our regiment carries a sword,' struck the sergeant dumb.

By now the peacetime engagements were increasing and military band programmes broadcast by the BBC were more varied. During the next decade such programmes as 'Bandstand', 'Music While You Work', 'Marching and Waltzing' and 'Friday Night is Music Night' all, at times, featured the Band of The Life Guards. In August and September, 1950, the Band performed mounted at the Edinburgh Tattoo in State Dress.

Having moved back with their own Regiment in October, 1951, the Band were, until March, 1952, billeted with C Squadron at the Imperial Service College in Alma Road, Windsor, which was a five-minute walk from Combermere where the rest of the Regiment were. The duty trumpeter at Combermere had to blow reveille four or five times in Combermere, starting at 6.10 am, then walk to the Service College and rouse C Squadron. There were occasions when some enterprising trumpeters not only used a bicycle to travel to the Service college but would cycle between the college buildings, sounding reveille mounted.

At this time afternoon practice for the younger members of the Band was still, as it had been for many years, a part of the daily routine. This practice, usually taken by the Band Orderly Corporal with occasional visits by the Director of Music, was known as 'Young Hands' and continued as part of the routine until about 1956.

In March, 1952, the Regiment moved to Wolfenbuttel, Germany, and the Band moved to Knightsbridge except for three trumpeters, A. E. D'Arcy, J. Rudge and E. Lowe, who went with the Regiment. Shortly after the move to Knightsbridge the mounted band were engaged to play

The International Horse Show, White City 1951. Lt. Col. A. Lemoine.
Drum Horse Bonaparte K/DMR L/CPL E. G. Madden

at the International Horse Show at the White City. At the end of the final late-night performance the musicians handed their instruments to the fatigue party and prepared to ride back to Knightsbridge. Meanwhile, the Director of Music had dismounted and gone for some refreshment. The Band Corporal Major at the time was H.G. (Todd) Sloane who was quite a comedian and impersonator. His apeing of Lemoine was well known, even to the Colonel himself, who always just missed the performance and his 'I'll get you one day, Sloane' was something of a band catchphrase. Corporal Major Sloane decided to take the Band back to barracks and leave the Director to make his own way back. Eventually a refreshed Colonel Lemoine came to get mounted, which he did after putting one foot through a beer crate on his first attempt. Leaving the White City, he turned left out of the gate; the Band had turned right. Some two hours later, at about 1 am, a phone call to Knightsbridge from the Kensington Police told of a Life Guard Trooper riding down Kensington High Street in full dress. A rough rider was despatched to bring him back; the following day he was sent on fourteen days sick leave for having had a blackout. How different a result from that of Musician George Allwright who asked for some compassionate leave to look after his small child as his wife was ill. His request was refused and the next day Allwright reported to the Guardroom to begin his 24-hour turn as duty trumpeter. When the Guard with trumpeter was turned out for inspection at 10.25 am, Musician Allwright took his place on the right with trumpet in one hand and his young child on a lead from the other. He was immediately sent home.

The late 1940s and early 1950s had seen the start of many engagements which became annual dates. The Royal Windsor Horse Show was one such event. Another was the Ideal Homes Exhibition, of which The Life Guards were the resident band through most of the nineteen-fifties.

Nineteen fifty-three was a year to remember and for the Band perhaps the earliest memory of those serving at the time would be the months of February and March and the Canvey Island floods, for, while many of the troopers from the Mounted Squadrons were sent to assist in the rescue operation, the Band had to exercise the squadron horses each morning for an hour, starting at seven o'clock.

On 28 April, 1953, in the Home Park, Windsor, Her Majesty presented new standards to the Household Cavalry. The whole Regiment was on parade with swords, the armoured regiment carrying service swords. The Band were dismounted and in state dress. The following year one of the old squadron standards was to be laid up at Benacre Church, Suffolk, the family church of a former commanding officer, Colonel Sir Robert (Eric) Gooch. The Band were instructed to assemble at the Cherry Tree. The majority of the band, not wishing to miss an opportunity of a drink before the parade, decided to arrive at the Cherry Tree in plenty of time for a drink in the bar. They duly arrived to find, much to their disappointment, that the meeting place was indeed a cherry tree.

The Coronation of Her Majesty Queen Elizabeth II in June, 1953, was the first occasion of its kind in which a Life Guards Band had taken part dismounted. Lt.-Colonel Lemoine, as senior Household Cavalry Director of Music, was given the choice of his band being mounted or dismounted. He chose the latter, much to the dismay of the majority of the band who knew the length of the Coronation processional route. The order of dress for the Coronation was scarlet tunic, overalls, wellington boots and spurs, crossbelt, waistbelt with sword slings and forage cap.

The Band of The Life Guards, alone of the Household Brigade bands, contributed to the safety of the nobility at the Coronation Ceremony. Some weeks before Coronation Day three Life Guards band boys, Lawn, Frost and Walthew, marched with the Mounted Squadrons from Knightsbridge to Westminster Abbey and there, together with troops from most

After Christmas Lunch, Balaclava Camp, Egypt 1955
*On Left*   L/CPL A. E. Darcy TPTRS T. M. Crosland, G. R. Lawn
*Drinking*  CPL R. E. Hannell

units in London District, tested the safety of wooden planks, mounted on scaffolding inside the Abbey, where the nobility were to sit. This was done to orders shouted by a Sergeant Major of the Welsh Guards by jumping up and down on them. Obviously the possible loss of three boys would have made no difference to the efficiency of London District, but Her Majesty's Guards would have been sadly depleted if the testing had proved the planks defective.

Coronation-related events continued throughout 1953. One of the more unusual was the Royal River Pageant on 27 July, when the Band sailed from Greenwich to Westminster aboard the vessel *Ford Consul*, while the band of The Blues took part on the vessel *Fordson*.

With the Regiment leaving Germany and, after a brief stop in England for the Coronation, moving to Balaclava Camp, Fanara, in the Canal Zone of Egypt, they again took their quota of trumpeters, Lance Corporal A.E. D'Arcy and Trumpeters E.Lowe and F. Balaam. Lowe and Balaam were, in 1955, relieved by Trumpeters T.M. Crosland and G.R. Lawn.

In October, 1954, the Massed Bands of the Household Cavalry played for the International Football Match at Wembley between England and the World Champions, West Germany, and what an experience it was for some of the more football-minded musicians to be on the same pitch as such stars as Stanley Matthews, Len Shackleton and Billy Wright. That evening a very successful Band dinner took place at the Paxton's Head, opposite Knightsbridge Barracks. A large gathering of past and present members enjoyed an evening of eating, drinking and story-telling.

Three young members of the Band, Loyd Franklin, David Johnson and Tony Walthew, during the middle fifties often spent weekends at holiday camps. Franklin, a tall handsome young man, invariably won any competition at the camp for the best lover. After having served his time as a squadron trumpeter at Knightsbridge, he left the Army and later sang and played guitar in a club in Tangier, Morocco. He was soon introduced to the Woolworth heiress, Barbara Hutton, who lived in Tangier. Miss Hutton took an immediate liking to Loyd and, apparently, he to her. They lived together for some three years. Among the many presents she gave to him was a Rolls Royce embossed with The Life Guards badge. Loyd Franklin later married a pretty English heiress, Penny Ansley. Loyd and Penny were both killed in a road accident in Morocco in 1968.

David Johnson, in civilian life, was firstly sub-principal percussion with the Royal Philharmonic Orchestra and then a principal player with the BBC Symphony Orchestra until his untimely death from a heart attack in Tokyo while on tour with the BBC in 1990.

Funeral of Maj. Gen. The Earl of Athlone, Colonel and Gold Stick, the Life Guards, Windsor Castle January 1957

A British Tattoo was held in Copenhagen, from 30 September, 1955. The various participants were billeted in a variety of barracks and other buildings. The Life Guards Band, some would say, hit the jackpot as they, with their horses, were billeted at the famous Carlsberg Brewery. Drink was plentiful and free. With a large proportion of the band being old soldiers and not averse to an occasional drink, memories of this Tattoo are rather vague.

After the retirement, in 1956, of Band Corporal Major Sloane, who's position in the Band was 1st Bassoon, Trumpet Major Clarke succeeded him as B.C.M. while continuing as Trumpet Major and Musician Tom Thompson filled the 1st Bassoon chair. Tom Thompson's other talent was as a singer and Colonel Lemoine employed him as such during bandstand and other concert engagements. After leaving the Army, Musician Thompson joined the tenor section of the chorus of Sadler's Wells Opera.

In January, 1957, the Colonel and Goldstick of The Life Guards, Major-General The Earl of Athlone, died. His funeral at Windsor Castle was led by the Band in State Dress with muffled drums.

Later that year it was back to Edinburgh, where some members of the Band thought their end was nigh with frightened horses bucking and slipping on the cobblestones, too near the battlements of Edinburgh Castle for comfort.

Every now and then an exceptional player joins the Band. In 1957 Colin Parr was such a player. Within two years he was appointed to the position of Solo Clarinet by the new Director, Walter Jackson, who also promoted him to Lance Corporal. He was more than a worthy successor to such former clarinet soloists as John Denman and Pip O'Connor. The Band had the benefit of Colin Parr's exceptional playing until he left the Army with the rank of Corporal in 1963. On leaving the Band, he was appointed to the Orchestra of the Royal Opera where he stayed until appointed Principal Clarinet of the City of Birmingham Symphony Orchestra. Even with his high standard and ambitions, the Bath Tattoo of 1962 will be remembered for Colin Parr issuing clarinet reeds made from cigarette packets to all The Life Guards clarinetists. The never to be forgotten result was the sound of a squadron of ducks emanating from the centre of the Massed Bands.

August, 1958, saw yet three more trumpeters bound for the Middle East. This time the destination was Aden and the trumpeters were B.J. Frost, T.M. O'Neill and J. Barnbrook.

In 1958 the Musicians' Union complained to the Ministry of Defence that the fees being accepted by the bands for thirty players was below that

66

which could be charged for thirty civilian musicians. Consequently an agreement was reached whereby, in future, military playing-out bands would number twenty-five players but charge the same fee as was previously charged for a band of thirty. When the band of thirty became the vogue is difficult to say, but under Lieutenant Gibson in the nineteen-twenties The Life Guards playing-out band numbered twenty-five.

During the latter part of the 1950s and early 1960s, occasionally, if the playing-out bands of both The Life Guards and The Blues were away, a composite band would be formed of the remainder of both bands and used for drill parades at Windsor. On one occasion a composite orchestra was formed to play at a Life Guards' regimental cricket match at Henley. During the lunch interval a well-known officer pointed to the only french horn in the orchestra and said, 'I don't like that thing, send him home'. So off home went Musician Close.

The saddest event for the Band since 1926 occurred on 12 March, 1959, with the death of Trumpeter Peter Bennett, who died from injuries received when his horse bolted the previous day while exercising with the newly formed musical ride. Peter Bennett was a most likeable young man and was very much missed by the friends he had made in the Band and Mounted Squadron.

From orphan to Senior Director of Music, British Army was the story of Lt.-Colonel Albert Lemoine, OBE, 'The Guv'nor' as he was known. In October, 1959, this great character retired after forty-three years' service, including twenty-one as Director of Music, The Life Guards. So ended an eventful era in the history of the Band of The Life Guards.

Trumpeter Peter Bennett tragically died 12th March 1959

# CHAPTER 8

# After Colonel Albert

Who would replace the Guv'nor? The choice was a former Household Cavalryman of pre-war vintage, Bandmaster Walter Jackson, Brigade Bandmaster of the Light Infantry. Only one of the newly appointed Lieutenant Jackson's former bandsmen followed him to The Life Guards, who could have been forgiven for expecting a sextet, as the former Queen's Bay was Michael John William Charles Laurence Maxwell Worthington, known throughout his army service as Max.

During his first year as the new Guv'nor the Band purchased a set of the long Bach trumpets which, having valves and a wider range than the Eb State Trumpets, could produce more intricate and varied fanfares in any key. On these trumpets the State banners are attached near the mouthpiece and over the valve casings, which differs from most regiments, who attach theirs nearer the bell end. The Blues, of course, use the same method as The Life Guards.

A concert in the Royal Albert Hall on 30 October, 1960, combined the Orchestra of the Royal Opera with the Band of The Life Guards in a popular Tchaikovsky concert conducted by former band clarinetist, Mr Colin Davis.

On 2 November, 1960, the Band arrived at Herford, Germany, for a month's visit to the Regiment. This proved to be an extremely busy month, with concerts in several towns, and quite a few parades. Time was still found to attend the several social events specially arranged for the Band. The most memorable was an 'Arabian Night' put on by the WOs' and NCOs' mess.

The Director of Music and four trumpeters, Corporal of Horse Bate, Lance Corporals R. A. Walthew and G. R. Lawn and Musician A. E. Close, flew to Chicago in September, 1961, to take part in a 'British Fortnight' at the department store of Carson, Pirie and Scott. As well as

# Einmaliges Gast-Konzert in Herford

## am Donnerstag, dem 17. November 1960, 20 Uhr
### Schützenhof-Stadthalle Herford

# MILITÄR-KONZERT

## Es spielt die Kapelle der LIFE GUARDS

(mit Genehmigung von Colonel The Hon. J. Berry, O. B. E.)

### Dirigent: Kaptain W. Jackson, A. R. C. M., p. s. m.

## Programm:

| | | |
|---|---|---|
| 1. Marche Militaire | | Schubert |
| 2. Ouvertüre | Die Meistersänger | Wagner |
| 3. Aufforderung zum Tanz | | Weber |
| 4. Polonaise | Ein Leben für den Zar | Glinka |
| 5. Kornett Solo „Nessum Dorma" aus Turandot | | Puccini |
| (Solis: Corporal of Horse Harry Dunsmore) | | |
| 6. Musik aus Aida | | Verdi |

## Pause:

| | | |
|---|---|---|
| 7. Auswahl aus | Flower Drum Song | Rodgers |
| 8. Wirbelwind Polka | | Cardew |
| 9. Walzer | An der blauen Donau | Strauß |
| 10. Eine Auswahl der Melodien von Robert Farnon | | arr. Duthoit |
| 11. Musik aus | Die Csardas-Fürstin | Kalman |
| 12. Marsch | Pomp and Circumstance Nr. 4 | Elgar |
| 13. Marsch | Alte Kameraden | Teike |

Regimentsmarsch der Life Guards
Nationalhymne der Bundesrepublik Deutschland - Britische Nationalhymne.

Eintritt DM 1,50                     Schüler DM 1,—

Vorverkauf: Städtisches Verkehrsbüro. Kurfürstenstraße 16, Ruf: 5841
Musik-Haus Rieger, Clarenstraße 22

On Parade for inspection of new no. 2 Dress, Knightsbridge November 1961
*Front Rank*  right to left MUSN's Bending, Cooper, Messenger, J. P. Walthew,
L/CPLs Ravenor, Andison, Cox, Lawn, French, R. A. Walthew, Parr,
CPL's Downs, Chessman, Cross, Harris, CoH Brown, CoH Dunsmore,
T/M Madden, SQMC Kennedy
*Rear Rank*  MUSN's Eden, Baldwin, Davies, Worthington

their duties in the store, the trumpeters appeared live on an early morning television show. The Director of Music, by now a Captain, had met up in his hotel with a Chicago Police Lawyer, who introduced Jacko to his police colleagues as a top British policeman. The Chicago Police afterwards honoured the Director of Music with the honorary rank of Captain in the Chicago Police. They had, by this time, discovered his true identity as his police card describes him as of the 'Kings Guards'. The American inability to cope with the English language was irritating to the trumpeters as they were always introduced as 'The Queen's Trumpeteers'. Having travelled 4,000 miles from Hyde Park, London, the trumpeters found themselves living in the Sheridan Hotel in the Hyde Park district of Chicago, courtesy of the US Military Police.

Each year now had its regular routine engagements and military duties. Visits to Bournemouth, Eastbourne and the Royal Parks were annual and the Trooping the Colour, Garter Ceremony, Lord Mayor's Show, Royal Windsor Horse Show and Royal Ascot were, in general, bi-annual. Of the new engagements, a week in Jersey in 1962 became a regular fixture. Engagements for the trumpeters included Lord Mayors' Banquets, the National Brass Band Championships, the Festival of Remembrance at the Royal Albert Hall and an annual visit to the Hyde Park Hotel for two trumpeters and a side drummer at the dinner of the odly named Guild of the Nineteen Lubricators.

Representing Great Britain at the *Festival International de Musique Militaire* on 1 July, 1962, in Calais, the Band were one of five bands taking part in a four-hour-long concert and a parade watched by an estimated 60,000 crowd. The other bands were: *La Musique des Equipage de la Flotte de Toulon* representing France, the 751st U.S. Air Force Band, *La Musique de la Flotte Belge*, and the Band of the Carabiniers from Holland.

Another visit to the Regiment in Herford took place in October, 1962. The visit included a short stay at Spandau Barracks in foggy Berlin, during which time a concert was given in aid of local children. A NATO parade and concert were held in Stuttgart, the Band of The Life Guards leading the parade, representing Great Britain once again. While in Stuttgart the Band were billeted with the US Army in Patch Barracks. The general belief that the American forces lived in luxury was soon dispelled when the Band living accommodation turned out to be one large room, full of beds with no spaces, each bed having just one blanket. What was near mutiny resulted in the appearance of pillows and more blankets, but no sheets. The Corporals' Club was more as had been expected, with The Life Guards musicians being privileged to order anything on the menu on the house; T-bone steaks, oysters and wine were the main orders.

Soon after returning to Knightsbridge the Band moved to Windsor to meet up with the Regiment on their return from Germany. Leaving the old Knightsbridge Barracks for the last time signalled the end of a tradition dating from before the First World War. Since that time, once or twice a week during the summer months, the Band would play in the barrack yard from 11am until 12am as an entertainment for the troops during grooming. The signal to begin playing was the eleven o'clock stable call, usually played by the duty trumpeter but on some occasions twelve trumpeters from the band would play a harmonized version of the call known as 'Massed Stables'.

This tradition was revived nine years later under Major Richards, and continued, spasmodically, during the Band's next stay at the new Knightsbridge Barracks and finally ended in about 1973.

During the sixties there were many incidents, the outcome of which, on looking back, were the basis of many a good tale. Three in particular had their funny side. Band Corporal Major Bernard Harman left the Band suddenly on being appointed to a tympani position with the Orchestra of the Royal Opera during the busy summer season of 1962. Lance Corporal Lawn was to take over as percussionist in the playing-out band for a fortnight at Bournemouth. On one concert the patrol 'The Wee Macgregor' was played. This piece was never rehearsed and so the new drummer had never seen or heard it. Half-way through its performance he turned a page to find that, of the next page, only the top half was there. On reaching the missing section, he stopped playing as did the whole band. After a bar of silence there followed, by the rest of the band, a vocal rendering of 'Rum tum tum, rum tum tum, rum tum diddy diddy rum tum tum' which was the missing side drum solo.

During Lord Mayor's Banquets, two State Trumpeters stand behind the Lord Mayor's chair and blow a short fanfare to announce each toast or speech. As their last note is sounded, two more trumpeters stationed just outside the dining hall repeat the fanfare as an echo. This procedure is totally unrehearsed and the echo trumpeters have no idea what the two inside will blow next. At one of these banquets a fanfare was played in unison, as is the custom, ending on a C, to introduce the Lord Chief Justice. When echoed, one of the two echo trumpeters hit a Bb at the end, which with the C of the other trumpeter was not exactly pleasing to the ear. The Lord Chief Justice, after his initial address, began his speech with, 'I hope I don't start on a wrong note'. Needless to say, the next morning four trumpeters were in the Director of Music's office, the outcome of which was an instruction that in future the trumpeters were not to partake of the Lord Mayor's port.

The third event was a very important service at St Paul's Cathedral, attended by Her Majesty The Queen and many other dignitaries. Eight State Trumpeters were to sound a welcoming fanfare for Her Majesty. Having left Knightsbridge Barracks by coach, ready dressed, leaving plenty of time for the journey to St Paul's, on reaching the top of Fleet Street and finding it completely jammed with traffic, a police escort was eventually summoned which led the coach down the wrong side of Fleet Street. On reaching the bottom of Ludgate Hill it was obvious there was no way through the densely packed crowd. Dismounting from the coach the eight trumpeters, in their splendid gold coats and cumbersome jack boots and carrying swords and trumpets, fought their way through the crowd and up the steps of St Paul's to find the doors closed and Her Majesty already inside. While standing and wondering what fate would befall them, an elderly lady arrived and said to the trumpeters, 'Oh, you're late too'. It was Lady Churchill.

One of the Band characters at this time was tenor sax player Corporal D. W. (Spud) Dodson, who, being an old soldier, knew exactly what he could get away with. With the Band marching along playing well-known marches, Spud would often play 'There's No Place Like Home' during the whole of the march and his very own version of the order to 'Quick March' always brought smiles to the faces of those receiving his order 'January, February, MARCH'.

One Sunday in 1962 The Life Guards were treated to a practical demonstration of the ancient term 'Follow the Drum'. A young drummer had arrived in the Band and on his first parade was one of two side drummers in the drum rank for a regimental Church Parade at Windsor. On the command 'By the centre, quick march', the drummer took his first step with his left foot. Never having marched with a side drum before, the drum immediately swung round the outside of his left leg, but, instead of correcting it, he proceeded to attempt to march out of barracks following the drum in a series of anti-clockwise small circles. Unfortunately for the young drummer, Spud Dodson was in the rank immediately behind the drums. Before he had completed two full circles the drummer was christened, by a very loud voice, with an unfortunate nick-name which stuck with him for many years.

Trade tests for all bands were introduced in 1963 and in May The Life Guards were tested by Lt. Colonel C. H. (Jigs) Jaeger, Director of Music, Irish Guards, while Captain Jackson tested the Irish Guards. The majority of The Life Guards passed as Bandsmen A.1. and so received a higher rate of pay.

In 1964 it was into a recording studio for the first time since the early 1940s, to record a long-playing record called simply 'The Band of The Life Guards'. On 4 May of the same year the Band lost the services of one of its outstanding performers when Corporal Peter Ravenor left. A brilliant euphonium player, Ravenor, who had been Trumpet Major of the 12th Royal Lancers, was also a first class performer on trombone, cello and string bass.

The most notable event of 1965 was the funeral of Sir Winston Churchill, in which Trumpet Major E. G. Madden on the drum horse

Alexander, and eight mounted trumpeters took part. On 14 May the Band led the Household Cavalry in exercising their privilege of marching through Windsor with Bands playing, having been granted the freedom of the Royal Borough that day. The parade, which should have been mounted, was instead on foot due to an epidemic of equine 'flu.

The regular flow of transfers into The Life Guards Band was steadily decreasing, which for the younger musicians, who had joined directly into the Band, was good news as it increased their chance of moving up and eventually getting a place in the playing-out band. It had long been the custom whereby band boys, young musicians and trumpeters were not encouraged to improve on their instruments for the simple reason that, if they remained less than proficient, they could be kept on the trumpet guard roll and thereby relieve the older soldiers of this chore. The establishment of the Band, for some time, had been forty-nine, including the Director of Music and four boys. Some time in the late 1950s boys were taken off the establishment of the Band and trained at the Royal Armoured Corps Junior Leaders Regiment at Bovington. From 1963 this training was taken over by the Junior Musicians Wing of the Guards Depot at Pirbright. The rank of Boy was now obsolete and the youngsters now held the rank of Junior Musician. The first Life Guards instructor of any subject at the Guards Depot was Corporal D. V. French, instructor of brass instruments. Corporal French, in his own words, got away with murder, as the Foot Guards ways were, as we have already heard, quite different from those of the Household Cavalry. On promotion to Corporal of Horse, French put more gold braid on the peak of his cap than the regulations stated, even though band NCOs have more than their equivalent rank in the regiment. The Guards Depot RSM could not understand why CoH French had more braid than he had. Corporal of Horse French also credited The Life Guards with several traditions of his own creation, which always worked to his advantage.

More new ground was broken in June, 1966, when the Band played the Regiment off at Heathrow Airport, their destination being Singapore. The Band then moved to Wellington Barracks to join the Mounted Regiment. The usual quota of three trumpeters had gone with the Regiment and they were Lance-Corporal S. Balshaw and Trumpeters K. Pollitt and R. White. Balshaw and Pollitt were relieved the following year by Trumpeters G. Rendell and K. R. Whitworth.

The Mounted Band disappeared in 1967 while rehearsing in Hyde Park for a review by Her Majesty The Queen and King Feisal of Iraq, to be held on 10 May. The Household Cavalry, with the exception of The Life

Freedom of Windsor Parade 14th May 1965, CoH J. L. Morris leading

Guards Band, had just finished their trot past and had left the parade ground. The Kings Troop, Royal Horse Artillery, prepared to fire and fire they did. Major Jackson, mounted on the most docile of horses, stood his ground. When the smoke cleared the Director looked round to give the order to march off, only to find that he was alone, the Band having bolted in all directions. One of the musicians, Bob (Geordie) Bending, eventually came to a halt in Kensington High Street. The order of parade for 10 May was soon changed to allow the Band to march off with the squadrons.

Trips abroad were plentiful in 1967, with the Band performing at the Berlin Tattoo, followed soon after by a visit to Brussels for a 'British Week'. The now well established custom of visiting the Regiment continued when, on 16 December, the Band arrived in Singapore. Broadcast-

Seremban, Malaysia 1967

*Rear Rank*   MUS J. Pinnell, MUS R. Bending, L/CPL A. P. Legge, L/CPL M. Rose, L/CPL R. J. Fletcher,
MUS E. Webb, MUS M. Nelson, L/CPL A. W. Hocking, L/CPL J. P. Walthew, MUS C. Jolley, MUS A. Nichols

*Centre Rank*   MUS B. Moore, MUS D. Halstead, MUS G. Taylor, MUS C. F. Corbett, MUS K. Pollitt, MUS I. Graham,
MUS M. Lucas, MUS J. Spencer, MUS T. Colman, L/CPL L. Davies, MUS D. Edwards, L/CPL S. J. Eden,
MUS F. J. Harman

*Front Rank*   L/CPL W. Marsden, L/CPL J. Henslet, CPL D. W. Dodson, CoH W. H. Chessman,
SQMC J. L. Morris, T/M E. G. Madden, MAJ W. Jackson, SQMC H. B. Dunsmore, CoH R. McDonald,
CPL R. A. Walthew, L/CPL B. J. Frost, L/CPL A. E. Close

ing on B.F.S. Radio and Television Sengapura and also visits to Malaysia and Hong Kong were some of the engagements undertaken before returning home on 10 January, 1968.

From the middle of September until the end of October, 1968, the two Household Cavalry Bands combined to provide composite mounted and concert bands. The latter continued with the usual round of engagements in Britain, while the mounted section went to the United States as part of a tattoo called 'The Queen's Guards'. The first place visited was The Spectrum in Philadelphia, where they performed from 24 to 29 September. Madison Square Garden, New York, was next with performances from 1 to 13 October. The final venue was Boston Gardens, Boston, from 15 to 20 October. The Military Band Pageant at Wembley during November included the Mounted Band of The Life Guards.

Band Corporal Major and Trumpet Major E. G. Madden retired from the Army in May, 1969, after 34 years, having held the appointment of Trumpet Major of The Life Guards for a longer period than any other, beating by 21 days his predecessor B. J. Clarke.

Tattoos and pageants were taking more space in the calendar and so, in August, 1969, it was back to the Berlin Tattoo, this time with the horses, four of which unfortunately had to be destroyed on the sea voyage.

When National Service finished, the days of specialist string players in the band also came to an end. Even in the heyday of the orchestra in the fifties, there were one or two double handed players able to perform both in the military band and orchestra, such as Musician Ken Dale; saxaphone and violin. Recruitment of double-handed players only began again in the late nineteen-sixties. Of the new breed of double-handers, two, Robin Bourne, saxaphone and violin, and Andy Morris, oboe and violin, subsequently became Band Corporal Major.

Major Walter Jackson retired in July, 1970, and his successor, Major Richards, lost no time in drumming up even more work for the Band in the form of civilian engagements. Although the extra income was welcome, travelling up and down the M.1 motorway soon took its toll and the turnover of band members was much above average. The band strength soon diminished to forty-three. One innovation introduced by Major Richards was the marching display, much disliked by his predecessor and by the Band. At a display at the Enfield Show there were no barriers separating the spectators from the arena, consequently some stray civilians somehow walked into the act. When the Band countermarched, this took the civilians by surprise. The Band then formed a circle, to find they had captured some twenty people.

Another new experience for the Household Cavalry Bands was Beating Retreat with the Foot Guards Bands on Horse Guards Parade in June, 1971. In September of that year a recruiting tour covered Keighley, Leeds, Bradford, Preston, Stockport and Manchester, which was followed, in October, by the move once again to Knightsbridge.

Corporal Major Harry Dunsmore retired in August, 1972. He was an outstanding player who, on joining in 1942, was immediately installed on the first cornet stand and at the end of the war was appointed solo cornet, which position he held for the rest of his service. A legacy left to the Band by Harry was the many cartoons drawn on the covers of numerous first cornet parts. Also in August, another of the Band's characters retired from the Army after 36 years' service, 21 of which were spent in The Life Guards. Before his promotion to Lance Corporal, Bob (Geordie) Bending, a clarinetist, was easily recognized by his arm full of service stripes. For many years Geordie was accompanied by Gus, his pet springer spaniel, who lived with him in barracks.

Outstanding was the result of the 1973 Kneller Hall inspection. This band was seen on television by millions watching the Cilla Black Show and by many more when the Band, massed with other Guards bands, played in 'Spectaculars' at venues all over the north of the country. Another visit to the Regiment in Detmold, Germany, brought their travelling to well over 10,000 miles in 1973.

The World Gymnastics Championships at the Empire Pool, Wembley, was new ground for the Band in April, 1974. Another stint at Royal Ascot in June was followed by a K.A.P.E. tour which meant six days in Bradford. K.A.P.E. is 'Keep the Army in the Public Eye'.

An enquiry was made as to the availability of The Life Guards Band for an engagement in France. The Band were available but were turned down by the French when they discovered that the Household Cavalry do not wear kilts.

The Regiment, although stationed in Germany, was sending squadrons for duty in Northern Ireland and in July the Band visited those squadrons in Armagh, to find to their horror the two squadron trumpeters brandishing S.L.Rs instead of trumpets.

The highlight of 1975 was a mounted band visit to Paris in June. A Remembrance Service at the Arc de Triomphe brought chaos to the Paris traffic and more chaos was evident at the first performance of the floodlit tattoo, as an article in the Regimental magazine, *The Acorn*, relates: 'The evening performance began at 21.00 hours and needless to say the first had its traumatic yet exciting moments. No one knew how the horses

In the Mess October 1970
CoH I. D. Gunn, CoH J. Henslet, T/M L. Downs, BCM H. B. Dunsmore,
CoH D. W. Dodson, L/CoH B. J. Frost

would react in a floodlit arena and everything seemed to be going well when, all of a sudden, the mount of Lance Corporal Morris shied at a shadow. The horse being ridden by Musician Ely decided that it was time to leave the formation and ended up (with its rider) in the middle of the arena on its own. Fortunately the rest of the show passed without incident. Naturally enough, the horse had its name taken. Appropriately it was called "Rodeo".' The final visit to the Regiment in Detmold took place in September.

Wimbledon and Paignton were the venues for another Guards Spectacular in April, 1976. Jersey was again on the calendar and the British Gymnastics Championships were on it for the fifth time. In September Musician Nick Slater and the drum horse Cicero were featured in the 'Blue Peter' BBC television programme.

'Band lets its hair down and enhances its image,' said the headlines in *The Citizen* newspaper on 26 October, 1976, when The Life Guards Band played at a brass band festival, 'Even the most dedicated of brass band fans who do not normally favour the brass and reed combination were bowled over. They admired the colourful spectacle of their scarlet uniforms, the State Trumpeters' opening fanfare and the well disciplined artistry of principals like trombonist Christopher Dean. The solo trombonist was brilliant with his velvety-smooth rendering of "The Way We Were" and his first performance of a James Last version of the beautiful Adagio theme from Max Bruch's violin concerto.'

Jubilee year 1977 was, as expected, a very busy year, with all the usual duties and engagements, plus many more as part of the Jubilee celebrations. The main Band engagements were :-

February – A concert at the Royal Festival Hall with other Guards bands raising funds for the Kneller Hall magazine *Fanfare*.

March – The Football League Cup Final at Wembley between Aston Villa and Everton. During the half-time marching display many of the Band lost their spurs and the second half of the match was held up while the search for them was made. It was apparently a boring match, as some newspapers the following day reported that the spectacle of the band searching for their spurs was the highlight of the afternoon.

April – Into a recording studio to record another LP.

May – The first visit by the Band to Guernsey, followed by a television appearance while playing for 'Songs of Praise' at Holy Trinity Church, Windsor. The last week of the month was spent in Edinburgh.

June – Trooping the Colour, the Jubilee Day Fireworks Display in Windsor Great Park in the presence of Her Majesty The Queen and the third big event of June, the Wembley Military Pageant.

July – The British Gymnastics Championships, then the Band's third sporting engagement of the year, the Benson & Hedges Cup Final at Lords Cricket Ground and finally a week in Eastbourne.

August – Another week in Eastbourne and, after a spell of leave, a week in Bournemouth.

September – The now annual visit to Jersey, followed by a Band social evening which was attended by many former members.

October – Tour of major towns and cities and back to the Empire Pool, Wembley, this time to play during a visit by the Soviet Gymnastic Team.

November – Wembley again, for the start of the Lombard R.A.C. Rally and also the long ride through the City of London on the Lord Mayor's Show.

By the end of the year the commemorative Silver Jubilee Medal, a personal gift from Her Majesty the Queen, could be seen on the chests of Major A. J. Richards, Trumpet Major R. J. Fletcher, Lance Corporal of Horse F. J. Harman and Musician C. J. Allen.

# CHAPTER 9

# Drum Horses, Kettledrummers and Drums

Drum horses have been a feature of the Life Guards from the day they accompanied King Charles II into London in 1660. They have mostly been animals of outstanding stature and colour. There are many paintings featuring drum horses of the eighteenth and nineteenth centuries, the horse of this period being generally grey or light brown. An engraving by Wenceslaus Hollar of the procession of King Charles II from the Tower of London, 1661, shows the Kettledrummer and Trumpeters of the Duke of York's Troop of Horse Guards, but the colour of the drum horse is not obvious. Half a century later W. Thomas engraved a scene of the Proclamation of King George I at Temple Bar, 1714, featuring a drum horse, but again the colour is not apparent.

In Her Majesty The Queen's collection at Windsor there is a watercolour by A. I. Sauerweid dated 1816 of a cream drum horse of the First Life Guards with drum banners completely covering the bowls of the drums in the manner used today when practice drums are carried. It could be that the drums were of copper and not particularly picturesque. The drummer was possibly John Edwards.

Three paintings by J. F. Taylor of about the eighteen-thirties show 'Palomino'-like drum horses. The Drummers are wearing the unique Kettledrummers' uniform of the Second Life Guards of the period and the drums are, in one painting, covered by the banners and in the other two the banners are draped to display the silver drums. Three drummers are thought to feature in these paintings, James Rawlins, William Batley and Cuthbert Blades.

An engraving by John Harris and painted by Henry Martens of the First Life Guards passing in review, published in 1865, shows a grey drum horse with all gold head collar, black beard and light blue background to the banners. The drummer is not using foot reins.

In 1887 the *Graphic* newspaper issued a supplement of an engraving of the Musical Ride of the Second Life Guards. In the background are the drummer and trumpeters and what little can be seen of the drum horse is obviously grey. A coloured lithograph after J. P. Beadle dated 1887, in the Household Cavalry Museum, shows the First Life Guards with a skewbald drum horse wearing a black over red beard. A Richard Simkin water colour of the First Life Guards horse c1900, apparently copied from a postcard photograph, is of a piebald horse with white shabraque, white sheepskin edged with red, with the beard white out of red. In a tinted version of the postcard the beard is white out of black.

The earliest photograph of a drum horse of the First Life Guards that can be identified is of D54 taken in c1895. D54 is its regimental number, the D signifying it was in D Squadron. It seems to be pale brown in colour and is ridden by Kettledrummer H. Smith. A photo taken two years later of Queen Victoria's Jubilee procession shows the Band being led by a grey.

In 1909 the First Life Guards had Paddy I, a skewbald. He was with the Regiment until 1916 when he was replaced by Paddy II, another skewbald, who continued in the Life Guards (1st & 2nd) after the amalgamation. His rider was usually Kettledrummer G. Carter who, like Paddy II stayed with the amalgamated regiment. Paddy II and Carter were the subjects of Sir Alfred Munnings' painting 'The Drum Horse', which was commissioned by Lt-Colonel Sir George Holford of the First Life Guards and presented to the Life Guards (1st & 2nd). Munnings also painted a smaller copy for Sir George, which is now in Anglesey Abbey, Cambridgeshire. Lt-Colonel R. J. T. Hills, the Life Guards historian, in a written article, referred to the drum horse painted by Munnings as Young Jerry. This seems to have been a nickname; he also refers to this horse's predecessor as Jerry. Beards were still varied; in the Munnings painting it is red and black mixed, but there is a photograph of the First Life Guards in 1918 with the drum horse beard all white.

Sandy is the earliest drum horse of the Second Regiment of which there is a photograph taken in 1896. The horse's colour obvious from its name. In the photograph it is ridden by Lance Corporal Kettledrummer Ambrose William Hulley.

During the reign of King Edward VII a mainly grey skewbald was used by the Seconds and was still in use on Lord Mayor's Day, 1912. This horse was usually ridden by Corporal Kettledrummer J. E. Hanrahan. Jack Hanrahan was later principal percussion of the London Symphony Orchestra.

L/CPL Ernest G. Madden on
Bonaparte and Trumpeter
E. Lowe.
The Life Guards 1951

T/M Ernest G. Madden on
Alexander The Great
c.1960

MUS Bernard Moore on
Hector c.1968

MUS Robert Newnham on
Coriolanus 1985

Kettledrummer Henry Smith First Life Guards on D54. 1895

Kettledrummer Alfred E. Morris, First Life Guards, on Paddy I c.1910

CPL Kettledrummer John E. M. Hanrahan, Second Life Guards, 1906

Kettledrummer Ambrose W. Hulley, Second Life Guards, on Sandy 1896

Kettledrummer William J. Grace, Second Life Guards, on Coronet 1921

In 1917, when the Band were in France, the drums of the First Life Guards were carried on a route march by a large, almost pure white horse appropriately named Whitewash. His more usual task was to carry SQMC Keilly into battle.

In 1919 Kettledrummer Western retired and the Director of Music, Lieutenant Miller, quickly signed up a well known orchestral drummer who was not the most expert of riders, so he was put through a hasty equitation course. His first parade was in Hyde Park. The Band moved off to the usual drum rolls which caused Young Jerry to rear up on his hind legs then, with the drummer clinging round his neck, he did the whole course to Hyde Park Corner at the gallop. He was eventually pulled up by a policeman. The new drummer disappeared that night and was never seen again.

King George V presented the Second Life Guards with a new drum horse in 1921. The horse was Coronet, a Hanoverian cream who, on the amalgamation a year later, was transferred to the 1st Royal Dragoons.

The Life Guards (1st & 2nd) probably had only one drum horse, the now famous Paddy II. No trace of any other can be found until George in 1931, by which time the regiment was called The Life Guards. George, a mostly brown skewbald, was the star of the thirties and died in 1938. When George performed as part of the Musical Ride he was accompanied by Marksman, a skewbald pony as a miniature drum horse.

George's successor was Jimmy, a skewbald gelding who had been a farm horse in Drumpt, Holland. Jimmy's first public performance was the Lord Mayor's Show of 1938. He was described in a newspaper article as 'gentle and loveable and a favourite with the ladies'. Jimmy remained with the Regiment until they went to Palestine in 1940. In 1939 a grey was used to carry a Guards-pattern side drum and Musician W. Ferris at the Trooping of the Colour ceremony. The last of the prewar Kettledrummers was Norman Harris who was also the last to hold the appointment of Kettledrummer.

After the 1939-45 war the first drum horse used was Pompey, of The Blues, who had joined them in 1938. He was used by both the Royal Horse Guards and The Life Guards until the arrival of Bonaparte in 1950. Kettledrummer Harris having left the Band in 1945, the first mounted drummer after the war was Lance Corporal Bernard A. Harman who shared the duties with Lance Corporal Ernest G. Madden. Early photographs of Bonaparte show him wearing a 1st Life Guards officer's

George, his Groom TPR J. Cookson and Marksman c.1935

Kettledrummer Norman Harris on Jimmy 1939

L/CPL E. G. Madden on ?Zombie, Earls Court 1954

shabraque, no drum horse pattern having survived the war. The beard worn was, by now, a standard Life Guards pattern of red and black mixed.

On the death of Bonaparte in 1954 two black troop horses, Emperor and Zombie, were used to carry the drums. Queen Wilhelmina of the Netherlands presented Hadrian, a piebald, to the Regiment in 1955. Hadrian was known in the Mounted Squadrons as Muffin. He had a habit of rearing up on his hind legs while carrying the drums and drummer. Due to his unpredictable nature he left the Regiment in 1956. Once again Zombie was pressed into service. Hannibal of The Blues was also used by The Life Guards until Alexander The Great had completed his training.

Alexander, or Alex, was a heavier and more cumbersome animal than his predecessors and started the fashion for the heavier horse which has continued to the present. Alex was a splendid piebald with a long white mane. In 1967 Alex, with Musician Bernard Moore, were the stars of a 'Blue Peter' childrens' television programme. Alexander The Great served

86

Hadrian with his Trainer CoH R. Hutton 1955

in The Life Guards until 1969, having led the Band and Trumpeters on many important occasions, including the funeral of Sir Winston Churchill.

Horatius, a former show jumper, began his training in 1962 and did his first parade, the Lord Mayor's Show, in 1964. On this occasion he not only wanted to lead the Band but also to trot in front of the Director of Music whenever the Band began to play. By 1967 it was decided that Horatius was not a worthy successor to Alex and so he was replaced by another skewbald, Hector. In 1969 yet another skewbald, Cicero, arrived to begin training. Cicero was later to emulate Alex and star in the television programme 'Blue Peter' with Musician N. Slater. An offshoot of the television programme was the publication of a book, *Cicero, The Queen's Drum Horse*. Hector, who was now sharing duties with Cicero, would occasionally go for a trot or canter as former Assistant Band Corporal Major Ron Lund recalls: 'After leading the polo teams into the arena at Smith's Lawn, Windsor, to be presented to Her Majesty The

Queen, the drum horse and trumpeters formed up for the playing of the National Anthem. As the Foot Guards band struck up the first note Hector took off, cantered round the perimeter of the arena and regained his position as the last note was played.'

Claudius began his training in 1973, only the third piebald in the Regiment. From this time The Life Guards had three drum horses until 1977, when the iron grey Coriolanus, or Bumble as he became known, arrived for training, making the total four. Cicero retired in 1979 and Hector in 1981. In 1986 Claudius retired and Coriolanus died. They were succeeded by a piebald gelding, Leonidas, who had been presented to the Regiment by Her Majesty The Queen. Completing his training in 1994 was Constantine, who is of the unusual colour of blue roan.

The Life Guards kettle drums, until recently, were carried on the horse with the larger drum on the right. This may be have been a legacy from former German drummers, German orchestral tympanists having their drums set in this way. Alternatively it could be that it is easier for most drummers, who naturally have a stronger right hand, to play the main beat, which is always played on the larger drum, with this drum on the right.

The presentation of the two pairs of silver kettle drums belonging to the Regiment is described in chapter two. These priceless drums, the head sizes of which are 22 $\frac{1}{4}$ inches and 24 $\frac{1}{4}$ inches, were modernized in 1982 to accommodate plastic heads and now have ugly chrome hoops.

The Regimental practice drums up to 1940 were of copper and from the late nineteen-forties until the late seventies a pair of aluminium drums were used. These were thrown out when the drum horse groom decided they had too many dents and a copper pair were acquired. Another pair of copper practice drums were made for the regiment in 1994 by G. Potter of Aldershot at a cost of £2,700. Practice drums are often used on non-state occasions when the banners are worn covering the whole bowl of the drum. The term 'kettledrummer' has been in use in the troops and regiments of Life Guards since 1660, from which time the appointment of Kettledrummer was a prized position. On promotion the Kettledrummer kept his appointment and would be ranked as, for example, Corporal Kettledrummer. The last appointed Kettledrummer left the Regiment in 1945 and from that time the appointment has lapsed, probably because 'no one thought or bothered about it'.

One of the most experienced mounted kettledrummers must have been Band Corporal Major Francis (Fred) Harman, who rode no less than five Life Guards drum horses from 1968 to 1988.

Cashier-Please Pull.....

Ⓗ P

Bin ___ 7 ___ Price N 200 NP

Author ___ LAWN ___

Title ___ MUSIC IN STATE ___
___ CLOTHING ___

Publisher ___ LEO COOPER ___

Source ___ 5DG0992 ___

Storage ___ FRI 165 ___

Subject _____

MUS Fred J. Harman on
Cicero with his father
B. A. Harman

L/CPL Fred J. Harman on

The earliest surviving drum of the Regiment is a side drum shell of the 2nd Scots Troop of Horse Grenadier Guards, 16 × 16 inches made of brass, c1710.

The bass drums have changed gradually over the years, from the 30-inch-wide shell with 24-inch heads as shown in a cartoon of 1849 by Richard Doyle, through the 16 ½-inch shell and 30 ¾-inch heads of the late nineteenth and early twentieth centuries, to the 13 ½-inch shell and 31-inch head used from the mid-nineteen-twenties, all of these patterns being rope-tensioned. The drum of today has a 12-inch shell and 28-inch plastic heads, rod-tensioned. No clear example of the emblazoning on the First and Second Life Guards drums can be found, but The Life Guards emblazoning is as illustrated on p. 91 and plate 14.

A Guards pattern side drum with drag ropes was used in the Second Life Guards, certainly in 1887 and probably for some time before that. Almost certainly a similar drum was used in the First Life Guards. At the turn of the twentieth century, shallow rod-tensioned brass side drums were in use. These were not emblazoned and were not used for important parades, the Guards pattern still being preferred.

During the First World War brass-shelled side drums, six and a half inches deep, became fashionable in most cavalry bands. These were emblazoned with the simplest regimental design due to their lack of height. The Life Guards took this pattern into use some time in the twenties, while continuing to use the Guards pattern. The cavalry pattern was discontinued in 1965, when a second deep rod-tensioned side drum was bought and emblazoned especially for the Household Cavalry's 'Freedom of Windsor' parade, the original Guards pattern having, by this time, been converted to rod-tensioning with false ropes. In the late nineteen sixties the Guards pattern drum ceased to be used. Four deep rod-tensioned side drums were issued to the Regiment in 1972 and were passed to the Band. The emblazoning on these drums was of a basic design of a coat of arms with a royal cypher on each side, the whole surmounted by a scroll on which was the regimental title. The wavy line on the hoops was white instead of the usual gold. The Band eventually had one drum emblazoned to regimental design. This was used only on important parades. One difference from earlier designs was in the title, probably due to artistic licence, the artist being a former Grenadier. Previous drums bore the title 'The Life Guards'; the new title reads 'Band of The Life Guards' following the custom of the Foot Guards who have 'Band' on their drums to differentiate between the Regimental Band and the Corps of Drums of the Battalions who have, for example, '1st Battn.

Side Drum Shell of Second Troop
of Horse Grenadier Guards c.1710

Cavalry Regulation Side Drum –
Bass Drum – Guards Pattern Side
Drum. The Life Guards 1922–65

Grenadier Guards'. A rod-tensioned bass drum was taken into use in 1976.

The following is a list of the names of as many drum horses as is available.

| *1st Life Guards* | | | *2nd Life Guards* | | |
|---|---|---|---|---|---|
| 1897 | D54 | | 1895 | Sandy | Sandy |
| 1909–1916 | Paddy I | Skewbald | | | |
| 1916–1922 | Paddy II | Skewbald | 1921–1922 | Coronet | Cream |
| 1917 | Whitewash | Grey | | | |

### The Life Guards

| | | | Regimental No. |
|---|---|---|---|
| 1922–c1929 | Paddy II | Skewbald | |
| 1929–1938 | George | Skewbald | |
| 1938–1940 | Jimmy | Skewbald | |
| 1950–1954 | Bonaparte | Skewbald | |
| 1954 | Emperor | Black | |
| 1955–1956 | Hadrian | Piebald | |
| 1954–1956 | Zombie | Black | |
| 1956–1969 | Alexander The Great | Piebald | LG130 |
| 1962–1967 | Horatius | Skewbald | LG150 |
| 1967–1981 | Hector | Skewbald | LG1 |
| 1969–1979 | Cicero | Skewbald | LG98 |
| 1973–1986 | Claudius | Piebald | LG3 |
| 1977–1986 | Coriolanus | Iron Grey | LG47 |
| 1986–1992 | Leonidas | Piebald | LG4 |
| 1992 | Constantine | Blue Roan | LG72 |

Household Cavalry Standing Orders of 1982 say;-
'By tradition, drum horses are to be named after classical heroes,' which prompts the question, who were Paddy, George and Jimmy?

The following is a list of as many kettledrummers as it has been possible to discover.

### Kettledrummers of the Troops of Horse Guards

| 1st Troop | Appointed | Known to have held appointment during | Resigned |
|---|---|---|---|
| Robert Mawgridge | | 1689–1692 | |
| Radman Simpson | | 1760 | 1767 |
| John Asbridge | 1767 | | 4-Feb 1781 |
| John Dressler | 5-Feb 1781 | | |

Kettledrummer Radman Simpson is buried in Westminster Abbey.

| 2nd Troop | Appointed | Known to have held appointment during | Resigned |
|---|---|---|---|
| Walter Van Bright | | 1681–1682 | drowned 1682 |
| Francis Brabant | | 1689–1691 | |
| Francis Hemrick Kister | | 1692 | |
| John Weitzen Miller | | 1759 | 28-Mar 1768 |
| George Malme | 29-Mar 1768 | | 8-Sep 1786 |
| Griffiths Jones | 9-Sep 1786 | | |

| 3rd Troop | Appointed | Known to have held appointment during | Resigned |
|---|---|---|---|
| Cornelius Vandenande | | 1689–1692 | |

| 4th Troop | Appointed | Known to have held appointment during | Resigned |
|---|---|---|---|
| John Bullaert | | 1690–1692 | |

## Kettledrummers of the First Regiment of Life Guards

| | Appointed | Known to have acted as K/D during | Discharged |
|---|---|---|---|
| John Dreslar | 23-Jun 1788 | | 25-Jan 1791 |
| Lassare Purnie | 23-Jun 1788 | | 27-Apr 1793 |
| William Jenkinson | 26-Jan 1791 | | 3-May 1793 |
| Benjamin Banner | 4-May 1793 | | 23-Aug 1814 |
| Thomas Robertshaw | 24-Aug 1814 | | 28-Nov 1816 |
| William McAdams | 29-Nov 1816 | | 13-Jun 1826 |
| Ferdinand Bies | 14-Jun 1826 | | Reduced 24-Oct 1826 |
| John Edwards | 25-Oct 1826 | | 13-Jun 1840 |
| Thomas Grist Snr | 25-Jun 1840 | | 9-Jun 1843 |
| Thomas Grist Jnr | 28-Jun 1843 | | 29-Oct 1861 |
| William Binnie | 30-Nov 1861 | | promoted 25-Mar 1863 |
| Jonathan Raugh | 22-Apr 1863 | | 4-Dec 1864 |
| Thomas R. Bannister | | 1872 | 1-Oct 1879 |
| J. Murray | 12-Mar 1882 | | |
| Henry Smith | | | 21-Dec 1895 |
| Harold Hamilton | 1-Sep 1902 | | 20-Feb 1905 |
| Alfred E. Morris | | 1908 | 28-Aug 1910 |
| Henry E. J. Moore | Oct 1910 | | 25-Feb 1912 |
| Henry Western | Feb 1911 | | 6-Apr 1919 |
| George Carter | 4-Jul 1919 | | 8-May 1927 |

## Kettledrummers of the Second Regiment of Life Guards

| | Appointed | Known to have acted as K/D during | Discharged |
|---|---|---|---|
| Griffiths Jones | 23-Jun 1788 | 1791 | 1793 |
| Lassare Purnie | 1793 | 1798–1799 | |
| James Rawlins | 2-Dec 1799 | | 7-Aug 1834 |
| William Batley | 1-Aug 1832 | | promoted 12-Aug 1834 |

| | Appointed | Known to have acted as K/D during | Discharged |
|---|---|---|---|
| Cuthbert Blades | 13-Aug 1834 | | 20-Apr 1842 |
| Thomas Beamond | 13-Dec 1837 | | 28-Oct 1840 |
| George Woolford | 12-Nov 1840 | | died 10-Dec 1840 |
| Edward Farman | 11-Dec 1840 | | 11-Feb 1845 |
| Thomas Grosvenor Atkins | 12-Feb 1845 | | 9-Dec 1846 |
| Edward Benson Erlam | 10-Dec 1846 | | 20-Apr 1852 |
| Frederick Woodhouse | 25-Apr 1852 | | promoted 19-Apr 1864 |
| Henry Barritt | 20-Apr 1864 | | 21-Feb 1872 |
| George Joseph Rawlins | 22-Feb 1872 | | promoted 25-Mar 1874 |
| Henry John Furber | 25-Mar 1874 | | 3-Aug 1874 |
| John Brown | 4-Aug 1874 | | 18-Sep 1885 |
| Alfred Halliday | 22-Feb 1889 | 1888 | 27-Mar 1894 |
| Ambrose William Hulley | | 1895 | 3-May 1897 |
| John Edward M. Hanrahan | 15-Feb 1899 | | 25-Jul 1914 |
| William J. Grace | 25-Jul 1915 | | 28-Feb 1924 |

## Kettledrummers of The Life Guards

| | Appointed | Known to have acted as K/D during | Discharged |
|---|---|---|---|
| George Carter | 4-Jul 1919 | | 8-May 1927 |
| John J. W. King | | 1925 | 30-Dec 1945 |
| Frederick C. Hodgkins | 1-Mar 1928 | | 16-Jan 1936 |
| Thomas S. R. Grisenthwaite | | 1932–1937 | |
| Norman Harris | 25-Jan 1938 | | 29-Dec 1945 |

With Kettledrummers no longer appointed, the following performed as kettledrummers during the following years:

| | |
|---|---|
| Bernard A. Harman | 1949–1963 |
| Ernest G. Madden | 1949–1969 |

| | |
|---|---|
| David N. Johnson | 1954–1956 |
| George R. Lawn | 1963–1964 |
| Bernard Moore | 1965–1971 |
| Ronald Lund | 1970–1984 |
| Francis J. Harman | 1968–1988 |
| Nicholas A. Slater | 1973–1977 |
| Brian L. Tibbles | 1973–1978 |
| Alan Roberts | 1974 |
| Robert Newnham | 1980–1986 |
| Phillip D. Lazenbury | 1984 |
| Simon J. Bolstridge | 1988–1994 |
| Nigel D. Maher | 1992 |
| Paul D'Arcy | 1992– |
| Justin Matthews | 1994– |

Lassare Purnie was the only Kettledrummer to have served in both regiments of Life Guards. He also served in the First Troop of Horse Guards. Not all the Kettledrummers have been drummers in the Band. In some cases other instrumentalists such as H. E. J. Moore, First Life Guards, who was principal bassoon, N. Maher and P. Lazenbury, both clarinetists, have performed as Kettledrummer. The latter was to become the principal clarinet of the Band. Corporal Saddle Tree Maker A. G. Barnes of the 2nd Life Guards, on the amalgamation in 1922, transferred to the 1st Royal Dragoons where he became Kettledrummer of his new regiment riding Coronet from his old regiment.

# CHAPTER 10

# The Bandmasters and Directors of Music

The earliest reference to a Music Master is in the orders of the First Life Guards of 29 August, 1795, which say: 'During the absence of the Music Master, Trumpeter Schreiber will take on him the command and the direction of the trumpeters'. It has been suggested that Cambert, the French composer, was music master to a troop of Horse Guards in 1672.

Who the first soldiers were to hold the appointments of Bandmaster in the two regiments of Life Guards is not clear. The rank of Bandmaster Corporal, equivalent to a First Class Staff Corporal, was authorized in 1865, but the standing orders of the Second Life Guards of 1859 imply that Masters of the Bands were soldiers at least from that year.

From Standing Orders 2nd Life Guards, 1856:-

'Bandmaster.

The Master of the Band ranks as a Corporal, and must exercise over the Musicians a due authority; should any one of them behave with impropriety or neglect his orders, he must report him to the Adjutant, or – for a serious offence – place the man in confinement, to await the decision of the Commanding Officer.

'He has charge of the Music belonging to the Regiment, and will keep an accurate List of it.

'He will arrange all new music for the Band, and instruct the young Musicians in writing it.

'He will practice the Band from 10 till half-past 12 o'clock every morning, and in the afternoon from 2 to 3 o'clock, he will give instructions to such of the Musicians as are not competent to creditably play their parts with the Band.

'Once a week he is to carefully examine the musical instruments, and at once report any loss or damage done thereto which he may discover.

'He will take the direction of the Commanding Officer, relative to any new Music or Instruments that may be required.

'The Band, or any part thereof, will not be permitted to undertake any private engagement without the sanction of the Commanding Officer having been previously obtained, and should that indulgence at any time have been granted, and Regimental duty afterwards found to interfere, such permission to undertake the private engagement will be cancelled.

'He will take charge of the Band in all situations, and will parade the Musicians every morning before practice, to see that they are properly dressed, clean and soldierlike in every respect.

'He will sign all Applications for Leave for the Band, previous to their being submitted to the Commanding Officer.

'When the Regiment changes Quarters he is responsible that the Music, &c., is properly packed, loaded, and safely deposited in the New Quarters.'

On 1 July, 1881, all bandmasters who had passed the Kneller Hall examination were promoted to warrant rank and this continued in the Life Guards, with one exception, until 1919 when George Miller and Charles Hall were appointed Directors of Music. The exception was Hall, who had been promoted to 2nd Lieutenant as Senior Bandmaster of the Household Cavalry in 1905.

For many years it has been accepted that Herr Bies was the earliest bandmaster of the First Life Guards whose name was known and that his successor was one Signor Ulrici, both civilians. Bies' term of office was said to be 1820–1830 and Ulrici 1830–1832. Bies was supposed, previous to joining the First Life Guards, to have been a member of the Duke of Kent's Band. There are, in the records of the First Life Guards, two soldier musicians of the same names.

### F. Bies *Regtl. No. 229*

Ferdinand Bies was born in Brunswick. He enlisted into the 1st Foot on 28 August, 1809, at the age of sixteen and married on 14 December, 1813. He enlisted into the First Life Guards on 25 July, 1823, aged twenty-nine and was appointed trumpeter soon after. On 14 June, 1826, he was appointed Kettledrummer, but was reduced (demoted) on 24 October, 1826, and discharged on 31 December, 1828, rejoining the next day. He was finally discharged on 23 May, 1832, because the Regiment was over-strength. His civilian occupation was given as musician.

MUS Paul D'Arcy
on Leonidas 1994

L/CPL Justin Mathews on
Constantine 1994

Side Drum. The Life Guards
1968 pattern

State Coat c.1800

Postcard of Trumpeter T. H. Graves.
Second Life Guards c.1910

## P. D. H. Ulrici *Regtl. No. 452*

Peter Diedrich Henry Ulrici was born in Hanover and joined the First Life Guards at Windsor on 9 May, 1832, aged 28 years and 9 months. He was discharged on 31 May, 1834. His civilian occupation was also musician.

## J. Waddell

James Waddell, one of the most accomplished bandmasters of his time, served as Master of the Band of the First Life Guards until 1863. Exactly when he was appointed is not clear, a report of his departure in the *Household Brigade Magazine* says he held office in the Regiment for twenty-seven years, having previously filled a similar post in other corps for a lengthy period. This would mean his appointment in the Life Guards being from 1836 but the previous Master is said to have left in 1832. The other corps mentioned is likely to have been the 80th Regiment of which he is said to have been Master of the Band from c1817. Again this is open to question as he would have been only twenty at the time. Mr Waddell died in his 79th year on 10 January, 1876, at 5 Holland Park Road, Kensington, London.

## J. Waterson *Regtl. No.1195*

Born in Blackburn in 1834, James Waterson enlisted into the First Life Guards on 5 September, 1853. He was a noted performer on the clarinet and wrote many works for the instrument. He rapidly rose to Corporal of Horse, which rank he held until appointed to succeed the eminent Master of the Band, James Waddell, in 1863. Two years later, on 1st April, he was promoted Bandmaster Corporal, the first to hold this rank. Waterson was a good friend of Gounod and the great composer would often visit the First Life Guards Band at practice. Bandmaster Waterson was discharged on 24 July, 1879, and became editor of *British Bandsman*. He died in 1893.

## W. Van Den Huevel *Regtl. No 1430*

William Van Den Huevel was born in Breda, Holland, on 29 January, 1836. He is thought to have been Bandmaster of the 9th Regiment of Foot in 1858. On 25 January, 1873, he joined the 7th (Queen's Own) Hussars, was promoted Corporal (Lance Sergeant) on 26 April, 1873, and Bandmaster on 19 July, 1873. He was appointed Bandmaster of the First Life Guards on 1 August, 1879; two years later, on 1 July, 1881, he was promoted to warrant rank. Bandmaster Van Den Huevel was discharged as medically unfit on 31 October, 1890.

### J. Englefield RVM *Regtl. No. 1627*

Joel Englefield was born on 18 November, 1844, at Maidstone, Kent. He enlisted into the 18th Hussars on 18 November, 1858. His first promotion to Corporal was in 1862, then Sergeant in 1865. In 1867 he was Acting Bandmaster of his regiment. He attended Kneller Hall in 1875, returned to the 18th Hussars as Bandmaster in March, 1876, and was promoted to warrant rank on 1 July, 1881. He married Ellen Cashal Crasy at Oxford on 8 June, 1878. On 1 November, 1890, he transferred to the First Life Guards as Bandmaster. His son, Albert Victor, served under him in the First Life Guards from 1901 to 1903 and continued serving until he was discharged as medically unfit in 1905. Bandmaster Englefield was in possession of three medals; the Long Service and Good Conduct, 1897 Jubilee and the Royal Victorian Medal. He was a well known brass band contest judge and lived at 22 Earls Court Gardens, Kensington. Englefield left the Army on 31 December, 1903, with a pension of fifty-four pence per diem.

### F. Haines *Regtl. No. 2469*

Born in Islington on 10 April, 1870, Frederick Haines enlisted into the Leinster Regiment on 20 April, 1884. He reached the rank of Sergeant before being appointed Bandmaster of the 2nd Battalion Kings Own Royal regiment, 4th Foot on 4 May, 1894. Eight days later he married Emma Victoria Blanche Heywood at Whitton, Middlesex, whom he probably met while at Kneller Hall. On 1 January, 1904, his appointment as Bandmaster First Life Guards took effect. Very little is known in the Life Guards about Haines, whose discharge on 15 October, 1907, at the early age of thirty-seven is strangely recorded in the simplest fashion in the Regiment. Bandmaster Haines was awarded the Queen's South Africa Medal with clasp 1901–2 and the Long Service and Good Conduct Medal.

Joel Engelfield RVM

James Waterson

Frederick Haines

George Miller MVO, MBE

## G. J. Miller MVO, MBE *Regtl. No. 2635*

The son if Major George J. Miller, Bandmaster of the Royal Marine Light
Infantry, George Miller was born on 20 January, 1877, in Secunderabad,
Madras, India. At the age of eight he became a chorister at St George's
School, Windsor Castle. His musical education continued when, in 1893,
he entered the *Königliche Kapellmeister Aspirants-Schule* in Berlin, where
he stayed until enlisting into the 4th Battalion 60th Kings Royal Rifles at
Dover on 20 January, 1896. George Miller soon found himself at Kneller
Hall as a Student Bandmaster. On completion of his bandmasters' course
he was appointed Bandmaster of the 1st Battalion Duke of Cornwall's
Light Infantry on 22 November, 1898. He was transferred to the Royal
Garrison Artillery on 1 April, 1903, with the task of forming an R.G.A.
band at Portsmouth. During his time at Portsmouth he also formed the
Portsmouth Operatic Society.

His appointment as Bandmaster of the First Life Guards took effect on
15 October, 1907. While with the Life Guards, George Miller made many
gramophone recordings with the Band which he raised to a very high
standard. He married a famous opera singer, Madame Cecily Gleeson
White, and in 1912 his book *The Military Band*, one of several he wrote,
was published. On 25 July, 1919, he was commissioned Lieutenant
Director of Music, First Life Guards. During his service with the Life
Guards he was awarded the Long Service and Good Conduct Medal, 1911
Coronation Medal, British War Medal and the Victory Medal. Lieutenant
George Miller, already a well known figure, further enhanced his reputa-
tion after transferring to the Grenadier Guards, where he rose to the rank
of Lieutenant-Colonel and was made an MVO and MBE.

Lt-Colonel Miller died on 3 February, 1960, and is buried in St Mary's
Churchyard, Farnham Royal. At his funeral the Grenadier Guards
provided a bugler and The Life Guards a trumpeter, G. Lawn.

Henry Eldridge

## H. E. Eldridge

Henry Eldridge, born 7 May, 1884, educated at the Duke of York's School, enlisted 1899 into the Rifle Brigade. In 1907 he began a course as a student bandmaster at the Royal Military School of Music, Kneller Hall. His first appointment as Bandmaster, of the 2nd Battalion, Durham Light Infantry, took effect on 1 October, 1910. While in the D.L.I. he played full back for the Regimental football team. In June, 1920, he transferred as Bandmaster to the Royal Garrison Artillery, Plymouth.

On 3 October, 1921, he was promoted Lieutenant and appointed Director of Music, First Life Guards. On the amalgamation of the two Regiments of Life Guards, Lieutenant Eldridge continued as Director of the Life Guards (1st & 2nd). His only medal was the Long Service and Good Conduct. He died while still serving, at the early age of forty-two, on 23 September, 1926, having suffered heart and lung disorders, and is buried in Highgate Cemetery.

Johann Gottlob Waetzig

## J. G. Waetzig

Herr Johann Gottlob Waetzig was born at Dresden in the Kingdom of Saxony of Swedish stock, his family having moved to Germany because of religious differences. His naturalization papers of 1850 state that he is sixty or thereabouts. He came to England in 1815 and joined the Prince Regent's Band at Brighton. After a few months he joined King George III's Private Band and continued in the bands of George IV and William IV. The Georgian papers of 1826 refer to Waetzig as: '1st Bassoon, £3–7–0 per week, 11 years service, 35 years old, married, four children, a most respectable man and the best bassoon player in England.' Waetzig's wife Christina was from Dresden, their four children were Johann Gustav who was a member of Queen Victoria's Band, Charles Adolphus, also in Queen Victoria's Band and later Bandmaster of the 3rd Prince of Wales' Dragoon Guards, Gottlob Alfred who became Queen Victoria's chief cook at Windsor and Augusta who ran a school in Brentford. In 1842 there was published a book which included some Life Guards Quadrilles by G. A. Waetzig. This could be a misprint for C. A. as it would seem unlikely that Queen Victoria's chief cook would have published a book of musical compositions. For eleven years J. G. Waetzig was civilian Bandmaster of the Second Life Guards, retiring in 1849. He lived at Surbiton Hill in the County of Surrey and died on 20 January, 1875.

Henry Angelo Michael Cooke

## H. A. M. Cooke

Henry Angelo Michael Cooke was born in London on 21 September, 1808, the son of Thomas Simpson Cooke, well known tenor, conductor and composer. From 1823 to 1828 Henry Angelo, commonly known as Gratton Cooke, studied at the Royal Academy of Music where he was later to be a professor of oboe. On 3 January, 1830, at the age of twenty-one, he was admitted to the Royal Society of Musicians. He was principal hautbois (oboe) of the Philharmonic and other orchestras, was also engaged at the English Opera House and at the invitation of Mendelssohn, a great admirer of Cooke's playing, performed at the Birmingham Festival. In 1837 he married a beauty of the day, Miss Kialmare, and lived at 8 Cecil Street, Strand, London. He was appointed Master of the Band of the Second Life Guards in 1849 and resigned his appointment in 1856. Gratton Cooke died at Harting, Sussex, on 10 September, 1889.

Carl Freidrich Hermann Froehnert

## C. F. H. Froehnert

Born in Saxony on 27 December, 1819, Carl Friedrich Hermann Froehnert came to England under the sponsorship of Prince Albert, probably in 1845 when he became Bandmaster of the 64th Regiment. Later the same year he moved to the 94th Regiment. About 1855 he became a naturalized British subject. In 1856 Froehnert was appointed Bandmaster of the Second Life Guards. While in London he lived at 19 Alexander Square, Brompton. He was admitted to the Royal Society of Musicians on 2 June, 1861, and is recorded as being a professor of the flute. In 1872, sixteen years after his appointment to the Life Guards, he exchanged positions with William Winterbottom, Bandmaster of the Royal Marines, Plymouth. According to the Marines, Froehnert had a particular dislike of wearing uniform and did not wear Marine uniform until 1883, although he had worn Life Guards uniform prior to 1872, as the photograph of him shows. He stayed with the Royal Marines until his death on 23 February 1890. He was buried with full military honours in Plymouth Cemetery.

William Winterbottom

### W. Winterbottom *1st Life Guards Regtl. No. 462*

William Winterbottom was born on 29 May, 1821, the son of J. Winterbottom who was Regimental Corporal Major of the First Life Guards from 1827 to 1839. Young William enlisted into his father's regiment on 29 August, 1832, at the age of eleven years and three months, and four feet six inches tall. He was put into Captain The Hon. A. C. Leggie's troop on half man's pay. By the time he reached the rank of Trooper he had six years' and nine months' service. On 12 April, 1843, he was appointed Trumpet Major but resigned his appointment on 24 July, 1853, and reverted to the rank of Corporal of Horse. In 1849, on 1 July, he was admitted to the Royal Society of Musicians. His marriage on 19 June, 1843, produced three children. On 15 August, 1855, he left the First Life Guards at his own request.

Sometime in 1857 William was appointed Master of the Band of the Royal Marines, Woolwich Division, and in 1870, on the death of his brother Thomas, succeeded him as Bandmaster of the Royal Marines, Plymouth. There he remained until 1872 when he exchanged positions with Carl Froehnert, Bandmaster of the Second Life Guards.

William Winterbottom was a versatile performer, playing the violin and trombone. He was sometime principal trombone of the Royal Italian Opera, the Philharmonic and other orchestras and was editor of *Chapell's Army Journal*. On 31 December, 1886, he finally retired from the Army and died three years later in 1889.

Carli Zoeller

## C. Zoeller *Regtl. No. 1522*

Carli Zoeller was born in Berlin on 28 March, 1840. He studied music at the Berlin Conservatorium under Hubert Ries, W. Garich and Grell, for violin, harmony and counterpoint respectively, he also played the flute. He travelled for a time in Germany with an Italian opera troupe before settling in London in 1873. On 25 September, 1879, he enlisted as a Private in the 7th (Queens Own) Hussars and was appointed Bandmaster the same day. He was promoted to Warrant Officer on 1 July, 1881. In 1884 he was elected a member of the Accademia di St Cecilia of Rome and, in 1885, a similar honour was conferred on him by the Instituto Musicale di Firenze.

Zoeller's great love was the viola d'amore and he spent many hours in foreign museums copying music for it. He composed many pieces for the instrument, several of which were published, one being Veneta opus 141, a legend for voice, viola d'amore and piano. He wrote a method preceded by a concise history of the instrument and its origin entitled *The Viola d'Amore, its Origins, History and Art of Playing It*. In March, 1889, he wrote an admirable lecture on the viola d'amore which was read at a meeting of the Cremona Society, illustrated by many instruments and accessories of which a catalogue was published by the Society. His many compositions include a comic operetta, 'The Missing Heir', a lyrical drama, 'Mary Stuart of Fotheringay' and a scene for soprano and orchestra, 'The Rhine King,s Daughter'. He also wrote four overtures and a violin concerto.

On 1 January, 1887, he was appointed Bandmaster of the Second Life Guards, a post for which he was well suited musically and would certainly have not looked out of place as he was a giant of six feet, four inches. Tragically he died two years later on 10 July, 1889, of heart failure after an operation for peritonitis, which was the result of an accident while taking part in the Military Tournament at the Agricultural Hall, Islington. At the time of his death he was editor of the *United Services Band Journal*.

Leonard Barker

**L. Barker** *Regtl. No's R.A. 18308 2nd Dgns. 2439*

Born in Brimington near Chesterfield, Derbyshire, on 21 January, 1852, Leonard Barker enlisted into the Royal Artillery at Woolwich on his birthday in 1870 in the rank of Gunner. On 1 May, 1875, he was transferred to the Coastal Brigade, still in the rank of Gunner but presumably working as a bandsman. He was appointed Musician on 22 November, 1876, was transferred to the district staff 1 July, 1877, and re-engaged on 15 August, 1881, to complete 21 years. On 1 November, 1882, he was promoted Warrant Officer and appointed Bandmaster of the Second Dragoons, Royal Scots Greys, which position he held for seven years until appointed to a similar position in the Second Life Guards on 17 August, 1889. Leonard Barker was a prolific composer and arranger for military band. He retired from the Army on 31 December, 1895.

Charles William Hemphill Hall MVO

## C. W. H. Hall MVO

Charles William Hemphill Hall was born on 13 September, 1858, at Georgetown, Bermuda, the son of a soldier serving in the Cameronians who had also served in the Grenadier Guards, as did his father who fought at Waterloo. Charles Hall was educated at the Duke of York's School. On 10 September, 1872, he enlisted into the Twelfth Lancers and was promoted Lance Corporal on 1 July, 1881, Corporal 8 November, 1882, and Lance Sergeant 17 March, 1883. On 27 August, 1884, he was appointed Bandmaster of the First Royal Dragoons. Two years later he married Nellie Ann Webb at Dundalk and they had seven children.

His long career in the Household Cavalry began with his appointment as Bandmaster of the Second Life Guards on 31 December, 1895. As senior Household Cavalry Bandmaster he was commissioned 2nd Lieutenant on 25 January, 1905. In 1908 the King made him MVO 5th Class. The newly established appointment of Director of Music coincided with his promotion to Hon. Lieutenant on 6 June, 1914. Further promotions to Captain, 25 January, 1915, Brevet Major, 25 January, 1911, and Major, 6 August, 1918, followed. During his army service he was awarded the Jubilee 1897, Royal Victorian, Coronation 1911, Long Service and Good Conduct, British War and Victory Medals.

On the amalgamation of the First and Second Life Guards in 1922 Major Hall continued in the new Regiment but not as Director of Music. He died later the same year on 26 October at Bedford Park, London, and is buried in the churchyard of Chiswick Parish Church. Major Hall's funeral was of a private nature but was notable for the many connected with his military career who assembled to pay their last respects. These included Lt-Colonel Rogan, late Director of Music Coldstream Guards, Lieutenant H. Eldridge, Life Guards (1st & 2nd), Flight Lieutenant Amers, RAF, and representatives from all bands of the Household Cavalry and Foot Guards. There were also many old bandsmen of the Second Life Guards present.

### W. J. Gibson *R.H.G. Regtl. No. 1381*

William James Gibson was born at Brighton in October, 1871. At the age of fourteen he joined the Royal Horse Guards (Blue) on 15 December, 1885. As a Lance Corporal he entered Kneller Hall for a Student Bandmaster course in 1889 and on 16 December, 1901, was appointed Bandmaster of the Ninth Queen's Royal Lancers. During his time with the Lancers he performed at the Delhi Durbar of 1903 and was awarded the Durbar Medal, followed the next year by the award of his Long Service and Good Conduct Medal.

In 1922 he was appointed Bandmaster of the Royal Tank Corps and on 12 October, 1926, he returned to the Household Cavalry as Lieutenant and Director of Music, The Life Guards. He retired from the Army on 15

William James Gibson

October, 1931. Married in 1897, he had four children, William, Alice, Charles and Marjorie. Lieutenant Gibson died in 1957.

## S. S. Smith

Samuel Stephen Smith was born on 10 June, 1882, and on his fourteenth birthday joined the 19th Hussars as a clarinetist, in which regiment he attained the rank of Sergeant. From 1910 he attended a student bandmasters' course at Kneller Hall until 4 January, 1913, when he was appointed Bandmaster of the First Royal Dragoons. He married Maud Stoughton and they had three children, Bertie Stephen, Phillip Douglas and Joan Murial.

S. S. Smith was promoted Lieutenant and appointed Director of Music, The Life Guards, on 15 October, 1931. He was an expert horseman and revolver shot. During his army service he was awarded the Long Service and Good Conduct Medal, British War Medal, Victory Medal and the 1935 Jubilee Medal. He retired from The Life Guards on 9 May, 1938, and in 1945 became Director of Music to the Metropolitan Police in succession to Flight Lieutenant Amers, another former Life Guard.

Samuel Stephen Smith (see page 113)

## A. Lemoine OBE, *psm*

From the humblest beginning as a band boy, Albert Lemoine rose to be the British Army's Senior Director of Music. Born 9 June, 1901, at Southwark, London, he later moved to the village of Newbridge, near the Curragh, Ireland, from where he travelled to Stoughton Barracks, Guildford, to enlist into the 3rd Hussars on 23 September, 1916. Soon he was sent to the Royal Military School of Music, Kneller Hall, to undergo a pupil's course as a clarinetist. On rejoining his regiment in 1919 he saw service in Germany, Turkey and Egypt. In 1924 Corporal Lemoine returned to Kneller Hall to join the 'Wembley Class' as a student bandmaster. The Wembley Class is famous for having produced seven directors of music from its twelve students. While at Kneller Hall, Student Lemoine won the Sir Henry Wood conducting prize and first prize for choral composition.

Albert Lemoine OBE, psm

On 9 May, 1926, Albert Lemoine was appointed Bandmaster of the
12th Lancers at Hounslow. Soon he was in Egypt again, this time for
eight years. During his service with the Lancers he obtained his psm.
After twelve years as a Lancer he was, on 1 January, 1938, appointed
Bandmaster of the Royal Tank Corps which, being a secondary staff band,
was considered to be a step-up.

After only a few months he was commissioned Lieutenant and
appointed Director of Music, The Life Guards. He was promoted Captain
on 1 November, 1942, Major 15 November, 1947 and Lieutenant-Colonel
14 July, 1951. In 1952 the Queen made him an OBE. His other decorations
are the Long Service and Good Conduct, British War, Defence, and
Coronation 1953 Medals and the 1939/45 and France and Germany Stars.
He had married May Boddington in 1926 and had two children, Robert
and Daphne. Colonel Albert retired from the Army on 8 October, 1959,
and died on 19 April, 1974.

Walter Jackson, MBE, psm

## W. Jackson MBE, *psm*

On 2 December, 1927, Walter Jackson, or Jacko as he was affectionately known, enlisted into the Royal Horse Guards (The Blues) at Regents Park Barracks, a four-feet-eight-inch boy of fourteen and too short to complete his training which in those days was the same as a trooper's. Therefore his training was not completed until he was eighteen. He was, like his predecessor, a clarinetist and in 1931 was selected for a pupil's course at Kneller Hall, something of a rarity for a Household Cavalry musician at the time. He returned to Kneller Hall as a student bandmaster in 1939, the outbreak of the Second World War interrupting the course which would normally have lasted three years. He finally left Kneller Hall in May, 1945, on appointment as Bandmaster to the 1st Battalion North Staffordshire Regiment. Unfortunately for Jacko the Battalion had no band. He was then posted to the 2nd/5th Battalion Northamptonshire Regiment in Austria and given the task of forming a volunteer band.

After a short stay with the Fifth Northamptonshires he was recalled to Kneller Hall to teach the clarinet. The Royal Military School of Music was without Government grant at the time and so civilian professors could not be employed. This dull period came to an end in November, 1946, when he was appointed Bandmaster to the Queen's Bays. Thirteen years later the Bays and King's Dragoon Guards amalgamated and Jacko became a light infantryman on appointment as Brigade Bandmaster of the Light Infantry Brigade in January, 1959.

On 8 October, 1959, Bandmaster Jackson became Lieutenant, Director of Music, The Life Guards. Happily back in the Household Cavalry, he was promoted Captain in 1960 and Major on 14 May, 1966. In 1971 Her Majesty The Queen made him a MBE. His other decorations are the Long Service and Good Conduct Medal and Bar, the War Medal and the Defence Medal. On his birthday, 25 July, 1970, Jacko retired from The Life Guards and took over as Director of Music of the Junior Musicians Wing at the Guards Depot, where he stayed until 1 April, 1981.

Antony John Richards, psm

## A. J. Richards FTCL, LRAM, ARCM, LGSM, *psm*

Antony John Richards was born in Rochdale on 15 August, 1930. His early musical education was as a chorister at Manchester Cathedral. After leaving Stretford Grammar School, Manchester, he enlisted into the 13th/18th Hussars on 30 December, 1946. His principal instrument was the piano, but he played clarinet in the military band. During his time with the Hussars he rose to the rank of Sergeant and saw service in North Africa and Malaya.

After attending a Student Bandmasters' course at Kneller Hall he was, in 1956, appointed Bandmaster of the Lancashire Fusiliers. On 6 May, 1964, he was commissioned as Lieutenant and appointed Director of Music of the Alamein Staff Band, Royal Tank Regiment. He was promoted to Captain on 1 April, 1966, and in June, 1970, was appointed Director of Music, The Life Guards.

On 15 December, 1974, he was promoted to Major. He retired from The Life Guards in 1984 the holder of two medals, the General Service Medal with clasps Malaya and Cyprus and the Silver Jubilee Medal.

After leaving the Army Major Richards was appointed Director of Music of the Royal Oman Police Band where he reached the rank of Colonel. When on parade with the Police Band his two medals seemed lost among the glittering chests of the Omani officers. At the time he was commissioned he had also become eligible for the Long Service and Good Conduct Medal, which he neglected to apply for. In order to attempt to gain some parity with his fellow Police officers he applied for and received his third medal some twenty years late.

While in Oman he was responsible for designing and equipping the Royal Oman Police School of Music. Colonel Richards retired from the Sultan of Oman's service on 5 February, 1994. He was, by this time, sporting a chest full of medals, having been awarded four while in Oman. They were:- The Order of the Special Royal Emblem, the Glorious 15th National Day Medal, 20th National Day Medal and the Sultanate Meritorious Medal.

## J. G. McColl ARCM, *psm*

James Gerard McColl was born in Glasgow on 6 April, 1937, and joined the 9th Queen's Royal Lancers in January, 1959. In 1968 Lance Corporal McColl began a student bandmasters' course at Kneller Hall. His first appointment as bandmaster was to the Queen's Dragoon Guards in January, 1971. Four and a half years later he moved to Bovington as Bandmaster of the Junior Leaders Regiment, Royal Armoured Corps. The following year he was leading the Junior Leaders' hockey team to the league and cup double in the UK Minor Units competitions.

James Gerard McColl, psm


March 30, 1977, and Gerry McColl was commissioned into the Royal Green Jackets as Captain and Director of Music, The Light Division, at Winchester. His next move was to Hong Kong as Director of Music, The Brigade of Gurkhas.

After seven years in the green of a light infantryman, Captain McColl became a cavalryman on appointment in January, 1984, as Director of Music, The Life Guards. On 30 March, 1985, he was promoted Major. During his army service he has been awarded the Long Service and Good Conduct Medal and the Queen Elizabeth Silver Jubilee Medal. Major McColl left The Life Guards in September, 1989, to return to his native Glasgow.

## Major C. J. Reeves LTCL, *psm*

Colin John Reeves was born at Kempston, Bedford, on 22 July, 1944. He enlisted into the Royal Artillery on 11 October, 1960, as a trombone player and cellist, ending his time in the band as Bass Trombone. After

Colin John Reeves, psm

completing a Bandmasters' course at Kneller Hall he was appointed Bandmaster of The Royal Scots (The Royal Regiment) on 12 July, 1977.

In 1985 he was commissioned Captain and appointed Director of Music, The Scottish Division. The following year he became Senior Director of Music, Headquarters British Army of the Rhine. From 1987 until 1989 he was a gunner again, as Director of Music, the Royal Artillery Alanbrooke Band.

His appointment to his present position of Director of Music, The Life Guards, was in October, 1989. In September, 1991, he was promoted Major. Major Reeves holds the General Service Medal with Northern Ireland clasp and the Long Service and Good Conduct Medal.

## T. J. Cooper

Timothy John Cooper was born on 18 April, 1961, in Gloucester and at the age of sixteen enlisted into the Army as an oboe player. His first two years were spent in training at the Prince of Wales Division Depot at Crickhowell. In 1979 he began a fifteen-month pupils' course at Kneller Hall, at the completion of which he joined the Band of the 1st Battalion, the Gloucester Regiment. During his time in the Gloucesters the Band did a six-month tour of duty in Cyprus and visited Denmark, The Netherlands and Canada. In 1982 Bandsman Cooper was promoted to Corporal and posted as the Woodwind Instructor for the Junior Band at the Depot at Crickhowell.

Timothy John Cooper

In 1986 he went back to Kneller Hall as a Student Bandmaster, during which time he was sent to Swaziland to help the Swaziland Defence Force Band find its way through twenty-three African National Anthems. Towards the end of his course he won the Director's Prize for Conducting in 1989.

His first appointment as Bandmaster was in 1991 to the 1st Battalion the Gordon Highlanders. Under his bandmastership the Gordons visited New York, Poland and Italy.

As part of the Government's Options for Change policy, the Gordons' Band was disbanded in March, 1994, and on 31 March Bandmaster Cooper was appointed to the newly authorized position of Bandmaster, The Life Guards. He is in possession of the United Nations Medal (Cyprus) and the Long Service and Good Conduct Medal.

*Bandmasters of the First Regiment of Life Guards*

| | |
|---|---|
| 1823–1832 | F. Bies * |
| 1832–1834 | P. D. H. Ulrici * |
| 1836–1863 | J. Waddell |
| 1863–1879 | J. Waterson |
| 1879–1890 | W. Van den Huevel |
| 1890–1903 | J. Englefield |
| 1904–1907 | F. Haines |
| 1907–1919 | G. J. Miller |

*Directors of Music, First Regiment of Life Guards*

| | |
|---|---|
| 1919–1921 | G. J. Miller |
| 1921–1922 | H. E. Eldridge |

*Bandmasters of the Second Regiment of Life Guards*

| | |
|---|---|
| 1838–1849 | J. G. Waetzig |
| 1849–1856 | H. A. M. Cooke |
| 1856–1873 | C. Froehnert |
| 1873–1886 | W. Winterbottom |
| 1887–1889 | C. Zoeller |
| 1889–1895 | L. C. Barker |
| 1895–1914 | C. W. H. Hall |

*Director of Music, Second Regiment of Life Guards*

| | |
|---|---|
| 1914–1922 | C. W. H. Hall |

*Directors of Music, The Life Guards (1st & 2nd)*

| | |
|---|---|
| 1922–1926 | H. E. Eldridge |
| 1926–1928 | W. J. Gibson |

*Directors of Music, The Life Guards*

| | |
|---|---|
| 1928–1931 | W. J. Gibson |
| 1931–1938 | S. S. Smith |
| 1938–1959 | A. Lemoine |
| 1959–1970 | W. Jackson |
| 1970–1984 | A. J. Richards |
| 1984–1989 | J. G. McColl |
| 1989– | C. J. Reeves |

*Bandmaster, The Life Guards*

| | |
|---|---|
| 1994– | T. J. Cooper |

# CHAPTER 11

# Sport

Sport in the bands has always been dependent on individual enthusiasm, which has produced a number of regimental representatives in a variety of sports. The Second Life Guards were renowned as a sporting regiment and this seemed to carry through to their band.

The earliest regimental representatives of which there is any record are Trumpeters M. Ilberry and Smith at rugby in 1893, followed by Corporal H. Harman and Musicians Griffin and O'Reilly at association football in 1909, all of the Second Regiment. Also in 1909 there took place a football match between old soldiers of the First and Second Life Guards, the result was a 4–0 victory for the Seconds, two of the goals being scored by Musician Lufton, a soldier of thirty-three years' service. In 1911 Trumpeter Clifford played rugby for the Seconds team that won the Army Cup.

Musician E. Crisp of the Second Life Guards was a gymnast of some note and was part of the Regimental display team in 1912. Being by far the shortest member of the team, Musician Crisp invariably played the part of the team's clown.

Corporal of Horse Trumpeter H. E. Pridmore, Second Regiment, played in the regimental NCOs' winning billiards team in 1913 against a team from Finchley.

Lieutenant Henry Eldridge had, in his younger days, represented the Durham Light Infantry at football and, although no longer a player, his keenness for sport still showed in his willingness to accept any engagement with a sporting connection. Another Director of Music and sportsman was Lieutenant S. S. Smith, whose enthusiasm for horse riding and revolver shooting, both of which he performed with an expertise not normally expected of a Director of Music, was in no small way partly the cause of his premature departure from The Life Guards.

On 19 March, 1923, the Life Guards (1st & 2nd) association football team won the Household Brigade Junior Cup, beating the 3rd Battalion Coldstream Guards by 2 goals to 1 at Leyton. The Life Guards left wing pair were Musicians Hendry and Wakefield.

The only Musician to fence for the Regiment was Trumpeter Grisenthwaite in the late nineteen-thirties. In 1939 he was a member of the team that finished runners up to the Queen's Bays in the Army Inter-Unit Championship.

After the Second World War the first to represent the Regiment was the rugby playing pianist. Musician E. G. (Ginger) Aitken, who also turned out for the London Scottish RFC.

The first, and possibly the best, of the Band footballers of the forties, fifties and sixties were the Brown brothers, Dodger (Les) and Topper (Bob), both first rate footballers. Les played full back for Windsor and Eton FC in the old Corinthian League in the 1949/50 season.

Cricket is one sport which was usually the domain of officers, but Boy Dennis French, a young lad of sixteen, represented the Regiment as wicket keeper in 1950. Being the only other rank in the team, Boy French not only had to change in a separate dressing room but had to lunch on his own as the other players of both teams were nearly always officers.

Band and Grooms v Carlsberg Brewery, Copenhagen October 1955
*Standing*  Dane, CoH F. Secker, F/CoH A. Cottington, unknown, L/CPL G. Harris,
  MUS L. Downs, MUS D. V. French, Sadler C. Missenden, MUS J. Cox,
  unknown TPR, unknown TPR, L/CPL I. D. Gunn, TPR D. York,
  Sadler Richards

In 1955, during the Band's visit to the Copenhagen Tattoo, a Band football team composed of musicians and grooms played a match with the Carlsberg Brewery team. Much pre-match talk by the Band convinced the Danes that the Band team contained several professional footballers. Consequently, for such a 'big match', a large crowd turned out to watch their team, containing at least one Danish International, get, as they believed, heavily defeated. Straight from the kick-off The Life Guards swept downfield and within a minute Musician D. V. (Hank) French at centre forward had scored what would surely be the first of many. How right they were. When the final whistle was blown the score was Band of The Life Guards 1 – Carlsberg Brewery 12.

Two or three years later a football match was played with the RAF Central Band and was a fixture for the next two or three years, the RAF having the better of the exchanges. One of the stalwarts of the team in these matches was the Band secretary, Corporal Ian (Jock) Gunn, who saved many more goals than he let in.

In 1962 the author formed a Band Football Club and entered them in the Hanwell and District Football League, Intermediate Division. The club's colours were red and white striped shirts, white shorts and navy socks. Due to duties and other commitments of some of the Band players, one or two troopers were asked to play. In its first season the team finished eighth of nine with a record of :- P 16 – W 3 – D 2 – L 11 – F 10 – A 40 – P 8.

The team that played the first match, which was against British Railways Staff Association, was :-

Mus. C. F. Corbett

Mus. S. Balshaw      Mus. W. Marsden

Mus. H. Wood    Mus. G. Taylor    Mus. A. P. Legge

Mus. R. Lund     Mus. G. Wells

Mus. A. E. Close    Mus. M. Worthington    L/Cpl. G. R. Lawn

Results of the 1962/3 season were:-

| | | | | | | |
|---|---|---|---|---|---|---|
| Lge | 26–9–62 | A | Brit. Railways Staff Assn. | L | 2–6 | Balshaw 2 |
| Lge | 24–10–62 | H | Eastcote Wednesday | L | 0–2 | |
| Lge | 31–10–62 | A | Hanwell Garage | L | 0–5 | |
| Lge C. | 7–11–62 | A | Southall Station | W | 2–1 | Close 1 O.G. 1 |
| Lge | 21–11–62 | H | Royal Horse Guards Band | L | 0–1 | |
| Lge C. | 28–11–62 | H | Met. Police Trng. School | L | 2–4 | Meaghan 1 Edmonds 1 |

| Lge | 12–12–62 | A | B.O.A.C. | L | 0–6 | |
|-----|----------|---|----------|---|-----|---|
| Lge | 27–2–63 | A | Southall Station | D | 1–1 | Balshaw 1 |
| Lge | 27–2–63 | A | Southall Station | L | 0–2 | |
| Lge | 6–3–63 | H | Brit. Railways Staff Assn. | W | 2–1 | Spencer 1 Legge 1 |
| B.C. | 6–3–63 | H | Brit. Railways Staff Assn. | L | 2–3 | Wood 1 Spencer 1 |
| Lge | 13–3–63 | A | Royal Horse Guards Band | L | 1–2 | Eden 1 |
| Lge | 17–4–63 | A | Eastcote Wednesday | L | 2–3 | Davis 1 Pen Eden 1 |
| Lge/BC | 24–4–63 | H | B.O.A.C. | L | 0–5 | |
| Lge | 1–5–63 | H | Hanwell Garage | D | 2–2 | Bradley 2 |

BC = Boughey Cup

On two occasions two matches were played the same afternoon. No records of the remaining matches can be found. The club's home ground was the Granville Playing Fields, Slough. For the 1963/4 season the Garrison Ground, Windsor, was used. The goalkeeper for most of the matches was a non-musician, L/Cpl. later RQMC, Ray Cornish, who was joined in the team at times by Troopers B. Meaghan, K. Edmonds, B. Davis and F. Bradley, the latter having begun his army service in the Band. During the team's membership of the Hanwell League four of the Band were selected for the Regimental team, they were Sam Eden, John Spencer, George Taylor and Hedley (Eddie) Wood.

The following season, after a bad start, the more accomplished players in the team wanted to sign civilian players to boost the standard. The author thought this defeated the object of the club, which was to give members of The Life Guards Band a game, and so he resigned as secretary. The new secretary was Musician Max Worthington. Needless to say, the team finished second in the league, gaining promotion to the Premier Division with the following record:- P 16 – W 11 – D 2 – L 3 – F 66 – A 35 – P 24. By the following season interest had waned and the team dropped out of the league.

In 1964 a match was played at Stag Meadow, the ground of Windsor and Eton Football Club, between the old 'uns and young 'uns of the Band. The match was memorable for its casualties, first Corporal Gus Harris was taken to hospital with a broken wrist, followed by Musician Gary Cooper with a cut head, the result of diving into a goal post. A message was received from the King Edward VII Hospital asking, 'What the hell is going on up there?' Although through the seventies and eighties there have been many similar matches, none have been as spectacular as the Battle of Stag Meadow.

The Royal Eastbourne Golf Course was the venue for a Band golf tournament during the Band's annual visit to that town's bandstand in August, 1975. The winner was Musician W. (Jock) Sandell.

Three sportsmen of the modern era of particular note were B.C.M. Ian Graves, Trumpet Major Peter Carson and Lance Corporal Ian Stott. B.C.M. Graves first represented the Regiment at football in 1976. The following year he represented Kneller Hall during his year as a pupil at that establishment. After his return to the Band he played for the Household Cavalry Regiment until 1984 and for The Life Guards again on rejoining the Regiment at Windsor. He became the first member of the Band to represent the British Army, for whom he played two matches. Ian Graves also played hockey for the Regiment and during the Band's tour of duty at Sandhurst in 1987 he played for the Royal Military Academy. The Life Guards regimental hockey team goalkeeper in 1989 was Ian Stott who also occupied the same position in the Household Cavalry Mounted Regiment's team from 1990. In 1987 Musician Stott was capped once for the Army under 21 team and twice for the Combined Services under twenty-ones, having come to the attention of the selectors while playing for Windsor Hockey Club. His representative career was curtailed due to Band commitments.

Trumpet Major Peter Carson excelled at three sports, representing the Regiment at cricket in 1984 and 1985, winning the London District Golf Handicap Tournament in 1984 and playing in The Life Guards squash team from 1984. In 1985 he was runner-up in the London District under 25 Squash Championship.

In September, 1984, the Band took part in Exercise Lionheart in Germany, during which was held a 'Potted Sports Competition'. The Life Guards Band were the outright winners and received the Davis Trophy, which was a magnificent galvanized bucket containing six bottles of the finest NAAFI plonk.

The most recent of sporting Directors of Music are Majors McColl and Reeves. Gerry McColl's great sporting loves were rugby and hockey. A broken nose while playing rugby for the Queen's Dragoon Guards Band team convinced the then Bandmaster McColl to stick to hockey which he did with some success. Hockey not being a popular sport in The Life Guards, Gerry McColl had few opportunities to play during his appointment to the Regiment, but when called upon he represented The Life

Guards with enthusiasm and skill. Colin Reeves' forte is the more sedate game of golf at which, within the confines of his previous charges, he excelled when winning the championships of the Band of The Royal Scots and of the Royal Artillery Alanbrooke Band. So far he has not had the opportunity to prove his golfing excellence to be on a par with his leadership of The Life Guards Band.

# CHAPTER 12

# Records, Postcards and
# Tin Lids

Postcards showing the Bands, Trumpeters and Kettledrummers of the
Life Guards have been published in their thousands, in colour and in
black and white. Many early twentieth century group photographic
postcards of both Life Guards Bands are now collectors' items. Some
individual musicians also appeared on cigarette cards, while occasionally
some found themselves on the lids of sweet tins. The most frequently
printed photograph of a Life Guards Trooper on book covers, postcards
and all manner of souvenirs of London in the nineteen-sixties was in fact
a picture of Trumpeter Peter Scutt doing sentry duty as a trooper at
Whitehall due to a shortage of Troopers.

Postcard of Band of H.M. Second Life Guards in State Dress.
Knightsbridge c.1904

Postcard of First Life guards going to Church, Windsor c.1906

Postcard of Band of H.M. First Life Guards in State Dress. Knightsbridge c.1913

# Records

Bandmaster George Miller, very soon after his appointment to the First Life Guards, took the Band into recording studios. Records under Miller were produced on Vocalion, Winner, Bulldog, Beka, Zonophone, Scala, Imperial, Ariel, Coliseum and The Twin labels. Many of these recordings were re-issued under different labels. Lieutenant Eldridge continued recording for Vocalion and Winner, and later for Parlophone.

The Second Life Guards Band appear not to have made any recordings.

After the 1922 amalgamation Eldridge recorded with Parlophone until his death. Lieutenant Gibson and the Band continued with the same company until 1930, when The Life Guards Band began recording with Decca. Gibson also made many records for the Broadcast label.

Decca and Broadcast records with Lieutenant Smith conducting were made until about 1936, when the standard of the Band declined. No more records of the Band were produced until about 1941, when a series of recordings for Columbia were made under Albert Lemoine.

After a gap of some 23 years the Band once more returned to recording in 1964 at Watford Town Hall. Captain Jackson conducted for the recording of the Band's first long playing record. 'The Band of The Life Guards' on the Delyse, Envoy label. A feature of this record is the magnificent playing of the Post Horn Gallop by Corporal of Horse Harry Dunsmore. From that time many records were made by the Band at regular intervals, with music varying from marches to big band sounds, to accompanying a male voice choir. On the 1986 recording with the Cotswold Choir, the Band used a singer for the first time since the mid-fifties when Lance Corporal David Bole sang the Flower Song from Carmen in French and the Miserere duet from Il Trovatore, with a soprano, sung in Italian. David Bole continued as the Band's singer and was still performing in 1994. In 1983 Trumpet Major A. E. Close recorded all the routine field and regimental trumpet calls of the British Army, produced on a cassette by DR Records.

## *L/P Records, C.Ds and Tapes featuring the Band of The Life Guards*

| Delyse | Band of The Life Guards | Capt. W. Jackson | 1964 |
| Liberty | Crown Imperial | Maj. W. Jackson | 1968 |
| Decca | The Queen's Guards | Maj. W. Jackson | 1968 |
| Liberty | Concert | Maj. W. Jackson | 1969 |
| Phillips | The Wonderful Musical World of Ron Goodwin | Maj. W. Jackson | 1969 |

| | | | |
|---|---|---|---|
| Phillips | Salute to Karl King | Maj. W. Jackson | 1970 |
| Phillips | Marches and Waltzes from Russia | Capt. A. J. Richards | 1971 |
| Phillips | A Night at the Opera | Capt. A. J. Richards | 1971 |
| CBS | This Royal Throne of Kings | Capt. A. J. Richards | 1971 |
| CBS | In Concert | Capt. A. J. Richards | 1972 |
| CBS | The Godfather | Capt. A. J. Richards | 1972 |
| DJM | England Made Me | Capt. A. J. Richards | 1973 |
| DJM | Champions All (45rpm) | Capt. A. J. Richards | 1973 |
| DJM | Horse of the Year | Maj. A. J. Richards | 1975 |
| DJM | Soldiers of the Queen | Maj. A. J.Richards | 1976 |
| K.Tel | The Queen's Silver Jubilee | Maj. A. J. Richards | 1977 |
| Sunset | ABBA | Maj. A. J. Richards | 1978 |
| Mercury | The Pride of the Regiment | Maj. A. J. Richards | 1978 |
| Droit | A Soldiers Chorus | Maj. A. J. Richards | 1983 |
| Droit | Trumpet Calls for the Army | T/M A. E. Close | 1983 |
| Bandleader | The Massed Bands of The Household Cavalry | Maj. A. J. Richards | 1984 |
| Bandleader | Boots and Saddles | Maj. J. G. McColl | 1986 |
| Music Masters | The Band of The Life Guards with the Cotswold Choir | Maj. J. G. McColl | 1986 |
| Music Masters | On The March | Maj. J. G. McColl | 1988 |
| Music Masters | Crown Imperial | Maj. C. J. Reeves | 1991 |
| Sony Classics | Royal Salute | Maj. C. J. Reeves | 1993 |

# CHAPTER 13

# Stations of the Bands

Until barracks were built in the middle of the eighteenth century there was no permanent accommodation for the military. Before that time each troop was allocated an area in which to find billets, usually inns or houses of public entertainment. In 1670 the areas for the Troops of Horse Guards were:

His Majesty's Troop

In the Strand, the back side of St Clement's, Drury Lane, Holborn, St. Giles, Gray's Inn, Long Acre, Covent Garden and St Martin's Lane.

Her Majesty's Troop

In Horseferry, Mill Bank, Peter Street, Stable Yard, Petty France and James Street.

The Duke of York's Troop

Tuttle Street, King Street, Charing Cross (except the Chequer and Star Inns, reserved for orderly men), Haymarket, St James's Market and Piccadilly.

In 1821 a regular changeover of stations began, with the two regiments of Life Guards and the Royal Horse Guards (Blue) alternating between Knightsbridge, Regents Park and Windsor. The Regiments of Life Guards had, for some twenty years, been permanently in London apart from excursions to the battlefields of Europe. The barracks at Knightsbridge were built in 1796 and those at Regents Park some fifteen years later, so finally dispensing with the leased buildings in King Street and Portman Square which had of late been used in place of inns and other private dwellings.

*Stations of the Bands of the 1st and 2nd Regiments of Life Guards*

| Date of Occupation | 1st Life Guards | 2nd Life Guards |
|---|---|---|
| 14-6-1821 | Knightsbridge | Combermere |
| 6-1822 | Combermere | Regents Park |

| Date of Occupation | 1st Life Guards | 2nd Life Guards |
|---|---|---|
| 17-6-1823 | Regents Park | Knightsbridge |
| 8-7-1824 | Knightsbridge | Combermere |
| 2-7-1825 | Combermere | Regents Park |
| 4-7-1826 | Regents Park | Knightsbridge |
| 5-7-1827 | Knightsbridge | Combermere |
| 5-7-1828 | Combermere | Regents Park |
| 7-7-1829 | Regents Park | Knightsbridge |
| 28-7-1830 | Knightsbridge | Brighton |
| 9-11-1830 | | Combermere |
| 14-7-1831 | Combermere | Regents Park |
| 6-7-1832 | Regents Park | Knightsbridge |
| 5-7-1833 | Knightsbridge | Combermere |
| 10-7-1834 | Combermere | Regents Park |
| 29-12-1834 | Brighton | |
| 2-7-1835 | Regents Park | Knightsbridge |
| 2-7-1836 | Knightsbridge | Combermere |
| 1-7-1837 | Combermere | Regents Park |
| 11-7-1838 | Regents Park | Knightsbridge |
| 1-7-1839 | Knightsbridge | Combermere |
| 1-7-1840 | Combermere | Regents Park |
| 9-7-1841 | Regents Park | Knightsbridge |
| 1-7-1842 | Knightsbridge | Combermere |
| 1-7-1843 | Combermere | Regents Park |
| 1-7-1844 | Regents Park | Knightsbridge |
| 1-7-1845 | Knightsbridge | Combermere |
| 1-7-1846 | Combermere | Regents Park |
| 1-7-1847 | Regents Park | Knightsbridge |
| 1-7-1848 | Knightsbridge | Combermere |
| 30-6-1849 | Combermere | Regents Park |
| 1-7-1850 | Regents Park | Knightsbridge |
| 1851 | No change due to the Great Exhibition | |
| 7-4-1852 | Knightsbridge | Combermere |
| 6-4-1853 | Combermere | Regents Park |
| 5-4-1854 | Regents Park | Knightsbridge |
| 4-4-1855 | Knightsbridge | Combermere |
| 1-4-1856 | Combermere | Regents Park |
| 1-4-1857 | Regents Park | Knightsbridge |
| 7-4-1858 | Knightsbridge | Combermere |

| Date of Occupation | 1st Life Guards | 2nd Life Guards |
|---|---|---|
| 5-4-1859 | Combermere | Regents Park |
| 4-4-1860 | Regents Park | Knightsbridge |
| 3-4-1861 | Knightsbridge | Combermere |
| 2-4-1862 | Combermere | Regents Park |
| 1-4-1863 | Regents Park | Knightsbridge |
| 6-4-1864 | Knightsbridge | Combermere |
| 5-4-1865 | Combermere | Regents Park |
| 4-4-1866 | Regents Park | Knightsbridge |
| 3-4-1867 | Knightsbridge | Combermere |
| 3-4-1868 | Combermere | Regents Park |
| 7-4-1869 | Regents Park | Knightsbridge |
| 6-4-1870 | Knightsbridge | Combermere |
| 5-4-1871 | Combermere | Regents Park |
| 3-4-1872 | Regents Park | Knightsbridge |
| 4-4-1873 | Knightsbridge | Combermere |
| 30-4-1874 | Combermere | Regents Park |
| 28-4-1875 | Regents Park | Knightsbridge |
| 3-5-1876 | Knightsbridge | Combermere |
| 25-10-1876 | St John's Wood | |
| 2-5-1877 | Combermere | Regents Park |
| 1-5-1878 | Regents Park | St John's Wood |
| 7-5-1879 | St John's Wood | Combermere |
| 5-5-1880 | Combermere | Regents Park |
| 6-4-1881 | Regents Park | Knightsbridge |
| 5-4-1882 | Knightsbridge | Combermere |
| 4-4-1883 | Combermere | Regents Park |
| 2-4-1884 | Regents Park | Knightsbridge |
| 1-4-1885 | Knightsbridge | Combermere |
| 7-4-1886 | Combermere | Regents Park |
| 6-4-1887 | Regents Park | Knightsbridge |
| 6-4-1888 | Knightsbridge | Combermere |
| 3-4-1889 | Combermere | Regents Park |
| 2-4-1890 | Regents Park | Knightsbridge |
| 8-4-1891 | Knightsbridge | Combermere |
| 6-4-1892 | Combermere | St John's Wood |
| 9-10-1892 | Shorncliffe | |
| 13-7-1893 | Regents Park | Knightsbridge |
| 3-4-1895 | Knightsbridge | Combermere |

| Date of Occupation | 1st Life Guards | 2nd Life Guards |
|---|---|---|
| 1-4-1896 | Combermere | Regents Park |
| 1-4-1897 | Regents Park | Knightsbridge |
| 4-5-1898 |  | Combermere |
| 3-5-1899 | Combermere | Regents Park |
| 1-5-1901 | Knightsbridge |  |
| 30-4-1902 |  | Combermere |
| 29-4-1903 | Regents Park | Knightsbridge |
| 29-4-1904 | Combermere |  |
| 3-5-1905 |  | Combermere |
| 2-5-1906 | Combermere | Regents Park |
| 1-5-1907 | Knightsbridge |  |
| 29-4-1908 |  | Combermere |
| 5-5-1909 | Combermere | Knightsbridge |
| 4-5-1910 | Regents Park |  |
| 3-5-1911 |  | Combermere |
| 1-5-1912 | Combermere | Regents Park |
| 30-4-1913 | Knightsbridge |  |
| 29-4-1914 |  | Combermere |
| 10-2-1917 | France |  |
| 27-3-1917 | Knightsbridge |  |
| 4-8-1917 |  | France |
| 2-10-1918 |  | Combermere |
| 3-5-1921 | Regents Park | Knightsbridge |
| 18-7-1922 | The Amalgamation |  |

### The Life Guards (1st & 2nd)

| | | |
|---|---|---|
| 18-7-1922 | Regents Park | |
| 2-5-1923 | Combermere | |
| 29-9-1926 | Regents Park | |

### The Life Guards

| | | |
|---|---|---|
| 26-9-1928 | Regents Park | |
| 1-10-1930 | Combermere | |
| 25-8-1932 | Knightsbridge | |
| 11-10-1933 | Combermere | |
| 1-10-1934 | Knightsbridge | |
| 9-10-1935 | Combermere | |
| 14-10-1936 | Knightsbridge | |
| 13-10-1937 | Combermere | |

| Date of Occupation | 1st Life Guards |
|---|---|
| 12-10-1938 | Knightsbridge |
| 9-1941 | Combermere |
| 21-8-1944 | France, Holland, Belgium |
| 9-3-1945 | Combermere |
| 9-1946 | Etonian Club |
| 1948 | Knightsbridge |
| 5-1949 | Victoria Barracks |
| 10-1951 | Imperial Service College |
| 5-3-1952 | Knightsbridge |
| 22-2-1956 | Imperial Service College |
| 16-3-1959 | Knightsbridge |
| 11-1962 | Combermere |
| 6-1966 | Wellington |
| 10-1968 | Combermere |
| 10-1971 | Knightsbridge |
| 17-10-1975 | Combermere |
| 20-2-1980 | Knightsbridge |
| 15-2-1984 | Combermere |
| 7-9-1987 | R. M. A. Sandhurst |
| 11-12-1987 | Combermere |
| 1-2-1990 | Knightsbridge |

The stations listed here are as accurate as it has been possible to ascertain. Knightsbridge Barracks, Regents Park Barracks, St John's Wood Barracks and Wellington Barracks are all in London. Combermere Barracks, Victoria Barracks, the Etonian Club and the Imperial Service College are all in Windsor. In 1900 the cavalry barracks at Windsor was named Combermere. For the purpose of this list 'Combermere' is used throughout. Regents Park Barracks was sometimes referred to as Albany Street Barracks.

On the 29 December, 1834, the First Life Guards Band marched to Brighton, but how long they remained there is not known. Whenever St John's Wood is listed the Regiment was divided between St John's Wood, Kensington and Hampton Court, St John's Wood being the most likely station for the Band.

After the Second World War a new system for stations was introduced. With The Life Guards and Royal Horse Guards (The Blues) each providing a mounted squadron at Knightsbridge, the two regiments each took their turn abroad. The band of the regiment abroad became part of the Household Cavalry Mounted Squadrons at Knightsbridge, the other band being with its own regiment at Windsor. The Household Cavalry Mounted Squadrons later became the Household Cavalry Mounted Regiment.

The periods spent at St John's Wood, 1876–79, and at Wellington Barracks, 1966-68, were due to the demolition and rebuilding of Knightsbridge Barracks, sometimes referred to as Hyde Park Barracks.

Brief periods visiting the Regiment in Germany and Singapore, etc., were in fact postings for the Band and was their official station for those periods, although the Band Office, Main Library and Stores remained in the United Kingdom. These postings have not been listed as they were sometimes as short as sixteen days.

# CHAPTER 14

# Regimental Music

The origin of official regimental music in the Life Guards is obscure and in most cases unknown. The First Life Guards' Slow March of that name is said to have been composed by the Duchess of Kent, mother of Queen Victoria, and brought to the Regiment by Herr Bies. Milanollo, the Regimental Quick March of the Firsts, was written by Valentine Hamm in honour of two young Italian sisters, Teresa and Maria Milanollo, both accomplished violinists. The Second Life Guards used only one Regimental March, 'Men of Harlech', played in slow and quick time.

On the amalgamation of the two Regiments, Milanollo was adopted as the Quick March of The Life Guards, with the First Life Guards Slow March joined with Men of Harlech as the Slow March.

Programmes of important events of the nineteen-twenties, including the 1927 Presentation of Standards Parade, show the regimental slow march of the Life Guards (1st and 2nd) as being 'The Lion' arranged by J. Hartmann. This march is not mentioned in any regimental documents. One theory is that it may have been part of the regimental music of the 2nd Life Guards whose badge was the Royal Crest of England, which is a crown surmounted by a lion.

The Life Guards trot past to the traditional Keel Row. The slow rolls of The Life Guards have not been used since some time in the 1970s, when those of the Blues and Royals were taken into use by The Life Guards, probably due to some unknowing mind wanting everything the same. During the Directorship of Major McColl the quick rolls used when marching on foot were changed from a 'five-pace roll' used by all the Guards Regiments to 'two, three-pace rolls' as used by Rifle and Light Infantry Regiments from whence Major McColl came. After Major McColl's retirement they reverted to the more traditional 'five-pace roll'.

In 1970 Lord Mountbatten, Colonel of The Life Guards, expressed his wish that the 'Preobrajensky March' be included in the music of the Household Cavalry and played on ceremonial occasions such as The Queen's Birthday Parade. The Director of Music of The Life Guards at the time wrote: 'This is a fine march and is particularly suited for a Mounted Band when played in the following manner: Start at second bar and play sections one and two only, D.C. and finish at the third beat of the eighth bar.' In 1979 a letter from Regimental Headquarters confirmed that this march should not be included as an official march of The Life Guards.

The trumpet call of The Life Guards is the calls of the First and Second Regiments joined. One routine duty call peculiar to the Regiment is The Life Guards' 'Officers Dress for Dinner'. The following calls have a different meaning in The Life Guards.

Trumpeters Call is used as 'Warning for The Guard'
School Call as 'Sick Call'
Household Brigade Call as 'Fall In'

An unofficial march, 'Onward Christian Soldiers (Lloyd George)' arranged by Corporal Peter Ravenor to include The Life Guards' Regimental trumpet call, was first played when marching the Regiment to Church in Herford, Germany, in Novemember, 1960. This was probably the first time a hymn tune had been used as a march by The Life Guards since 1914, prior to which time hymn tunes were mainly played when marching to Church. The First Life Guards under Miller would march back to such tunes as 'I've been out with Charlie Brown' and 'Won't you come home Bill Bailey'.

Four Life Guard quadrilles written by C. A. Waetzig*, a son of J. G. Waetzig, were in 1987 brought to the attention of the Director of Music of the Regiment and in 1993 the score of the Horse Grenadiers' March was given to the Household Cavalry Museum. This march was apparently played at a review by H.M. The King of the Household Brigade on Wimbledon Common on 18 May, 1772.

* See page 105 (Waetzig biography)

*The Life Guards, 'Officers Dress for Dinner'*

Slow Rolls

The Life Guards

The Blues and Royals

# CHAPTER 15

# Dress

The uniforms of the kettledrummers and trumpeters of the Troops of Horse Guards are vague, except for the state dress. Before 1788 not much evidence is available as to whether there were differences in the dress of the kettledrummers, trumpeters and private gentlemen. There are many publications describing the uniforms of the Troops of Horse Guards and Horse Grenadier Guards, so I will not attempt to speculate on what was.

State Dress is another matter and has changed little in three hundred and thirty years. The coat, as illustrated opposite page 99, was worn by the kettledrummers and trumpeters of the Horse Guards and, apart from the obvious changes of Royal Cyphers, other small changes have been few. Firstly, in 1691 the silver lace was changed to gold and silver and then in 1699 was changed to all gold.

The basic coat was crimson with blue cuffs and no collar. Later a blue stand collar with sloping front opening was added, which was then made higher and fastened at the front, both versions trimmed with gold lace. Although the pattern of the gold lace has remained the same, its design on the coat has changed, particularly since the time of King George III. The lace on the sleeves is now straight round the sleeve, whereas it used to be chevron shaped. Similar changes can be seen on the back and sides. A narrow strip of velvet covered in gold lace used to hang from the back of each shoulder to the bottom of the coat. This strip now hangs from under the arm.

State dress, not being a Regimental uniform, was for many years provided and paid for by the sovereign. In the Great Wardrobe books of the seventeenth and eighteenth centuries are the description of, and orders for, clothing to be provided for the trumpeters and kettledrummers of the Horse Guards and drummers and hautbois of the Horse Grenadier Guards. It can be seen that the cloth for the Horse Grenadier Guards was of an inferior quality, the following extract also contains the first mention of the gold lace:

'2nd June 1691.
For One Kettledrummer and three Trumpeters Liveries unto Each of them these particulars following
A Coat of Crimson Velvett lined with blew serge and trimed with broad gold and silver arras lace and a gold cheque lace embroidered on back and breast with their Majesties Cyphers XXX R R & Crowns. A Crimson Cloth Cloak lyned with blew serge and trimed with broad gold and silver arras lace & the cape faced with blew velvett. A pair of Crimson Cloth Breeches. A pair of Embroidered Banners with their Majesties Arms and Supporters lined with blew sarsnett and trimed with gold and silver fringe with a pair of Trumpet Strings and Tassells for the Trumpeters, and for the Kettledrummer a large pair of banners lyned with blew serge, embroidered and trimed as the Trumpeters without Strings and Tassells. To each of them a Buff Belt trimed with Gold and Silver Arras lace. A Cordebec Hatt trimed with gold and silver open lace and band suitable.
A Black Velvett Capp And.
For four Hautbois and Two Drumers Liveries unto each of them.
A Coat of Crimson Cloth trimed with broad silk and silver lace and Black Velvett lace lined with blew serge. Embroidered on the back with Their Majesties Cypher and Crowne one pair blew Cloth Breeches one redd Cloth Cloake faced with blew serge one leather belt sticht with silver. One Cordebec Hatt laced with gold and silver lace and a gold and silver band. One Black Velvett Capp.
By Order of His Grace the Duke of Ormond.'

The Cordebec hat was made of a felt imitation of beaver fur, said to have originated from Caudebec in Normandy.

Exactly what shape the black cap was is open to conjecture, although an engraving of the proclamation of King George I in 1714 shows the familiar jockey cap with rounded peak. The cap worn now is blue velvet with a square peak. A new tricorn hat edged with gold and with gold loops and buttons called a Carolina, made from Carolina beaver fur, was ordered for the coronation of King George I. This pattern hat was still in use in 1750.

A painting of 1720 shows a trumpeter wearing red breeches with white knee pieces and high black boots. Charles Stadden in his *The Life Guards*

*Dress and Appointments 1660–1914* says buff breeches were worn with white knee pieces in 1750. According to the diary of the First Life Guards, jackboots and white pantaloons were first worn on 12 March, 1812, and have continued to the present day for the trumpeters and band. The kettledrummers and dismounted side drummers now wear hessian boots. Swan neck jack spurs are worn on the jackboots and, until 1939, on the drummers' hessian boots when in full or state dress. Since the end of the Second World War the drummers have worn the ordinary ankle or knee boot spurs.

A confusing order of 1802, which is in Chapter 2, page ooo gives the impression that the Band at that time did not wear state dress, yet a 2nd Life Guards order of 1 August, 1799, says:

'The Commander in Chief's Inspection
His Royal Highness Field Marshal the Duke of York having been most graciously pleased to signify his intention of being present at the exercise of the Second Regiment of Life Guards at Nine O'clock tomorrow morning in Hyde Park. The Regiment will appear powdered, and in full dress, Cloaks rolled, Black Bradoons, and Black Flounces, with the Old Furniture, MUSIC IN STATE CLOTHING.'

The belt worn circa 1720 was crimson laced with gold, as were the sword slings; the buckle was of gilt. Later the buff belt and slings with gold lace were taken back into wear. White gauntlets have occasionally been worn with state dress instead of short white gloves.

Some time between 1817 and 1832 a helmet with a red crest was worn by the Band and trumpeters in state dress. There is a painting by A. J. Dubois Drahonet of this dress in Her Majesty the Queen's collection in Windsor Castle. By 1865 the jockey cap was back in use.

From the beginning swords have been worn by the trumpeters. The pattern of sword was generally that carried by the troopers but sometimes with a shorter blade. The trumpeters of the First Life Guards from about 1830 to 1882 had their own pattern sword which was unique in the British Army. In an engraving of the First Life Guards of 1865 the Band are wearing a distinctive band sword. There is a group photograph of the Second Life Guards Band in state dress, taken about 1905, in which the whole band are wearing state swords; what the occasion or reason was is not known. It certainly has not been the practice for the Bands to wear swords this century and probably not for some time before.

From 1788 the Regimental uniforms of the Music and Trumpeters was not dissimilar to the troopers: a cocked hat laced with gold, with gold tassels and a white over red plume. The coat, including the stand collar was scarlet; the collar was laced with narrow gold lace; there were gold epaulettes, gold lace chevrons on blue cuffs; the skirt of the coat also had gold chevrons and was turned back revealing white facing cloth which was decorated with blue ornaments laced with gold. On the blue lapels were gold lace horizontal bars. Whitened buff gauntlets and crossbelts were worn. High black boots and what appear to be white pantaloons completed this order of dress. The pantaloons seem to contradict the orders of 12 March, 1812.

By 1816 the coat was a single-breasted coatee with brass or gilt buttons. It had a high gold laced collar with blue van dyke and gold lace epaulettes. The coat tails were turned back revealing blue facings. Two paintings by Sauerweid of the same period differ slightly; firstly a trumpeter has a plain gold crossbelt, whereas a kettledrummer has a blue van dyke through his, and he also has narrow gold shoulder straps instead of the elaborate gold epaulettes of the trumpeter. A yellow and red scarf (sash) was worn round the waist under a white belt with sword slings; white gauntlets and a black cocked hat completed the dress. The hat by this time had a red plume across the top from side to side, a short white upright plume at the front and elaborate gold lace across front and back. The cloak worn at this time was scarlet with a stand collar and a large, almost cape-like, blue collar. There were gold lace bars across the front of the cloak. Trousers issued in 1817 were of claret mixture, instead of the blue as had previously been worn, with a broad scarlet stripe down the outside of the legs.

The Regiments had, in 1812, been issued with helmets and in 1817 another pattern was issued. Probably the only trumpeters to have worn the first pattern were those involved in the Peninsular War and at Waterloo, the cocked hat not being abolished for the Bands until 6 May, 1856.

The trumpeters in the eighteen-twenties were wearing cuirasses and the giant bearskin cap taken into wear for important occasions. On the introduction of the string or cord for the crossbelt in June, 1829, the First Regiment took to wearing red and the Second blue.

In 1842 another new helmet was introduced, much like today's pattern. The plumes for the Regiments were white and for the Band and trumpeters red. The Life Guards in the nineteen-twenties took to making what is called an 'onion' at the top of their plumes. In the Life Guards the chin strap is worn under the lower lip, but brass and woodwind players generally rest the strap on top of their mouthpiece when playing.

NCO's First Life Guards c.1882. Trumpeter CPL I. Golding wearing the pre-1883 pattern band tunic

The scarlet tunic was first worn in the late eighteen-fifties and there were noticeable differences between the bands of the two Regiments. The First's band tunic had wide gold lace down both front edges which did not overlap when fastened by hooks and eyes; there was a row of small gilt studs down the centre front to the waist and the lace continued round the bottom of the tunic. Shoulder straps were identical to those of a trooper, i.e. blue – edged with gold lace and a gold embroidered I on the blue. The cuff was blue and straight across the top and braided at the top only, with ⅜" gold lace with circles of russia above. The collar was blue – edged all round with lace with circles of russia inside the lace. The Second Life Guards had piping of gold russia down the front which was fastened by brass buttons and also round the edge of the skirt which was cut away

Jenny Seagroves' 30th birthday present from Michael Winner –
The Band of the Life Guards in the new issue scarlet capes 1988

L/CoH D. M. Bole ready for ambulance duty

The Band at RMA Sandhurst 1987

MUS Pearson, MUS Lazenbury, CoH Poland, T/M Morris, MUS Dare,
MUS Newnham, MUS Allen, CoH Allen, SQHC Mean, CoH Bourne,
CoH Hopkins, L/CPL Gook, L/CoH Woodhouse, MUS Stott, L/CPL Collier,
MUS Bailey, L/CPL White, W.O.2 Whitworth, L/CoH Graves, MUS Dry,
MUS Carson, MUS Severn, L/CPL Dutton, MUS Hudson, L/CoH Young,
MUS Egerton, L/CPL Cox, MUS Morrish, L/CPL Bromley, MUS Everatt,
L/CoH Grieve, MUS Rickard, L/CoH Pankhurst, L/CoH Bole, MUS Clark,
Major J. G. McColl, BCM Harman

at the opening. The shoulder straps were gold plaited and the blue cuff shaped up to a point at the back. The blue cuffs and collar had gold lace of a design peculiar to the Seconds on the edges, very little of the blue of the collar being visible.

These two patterns of tunic continued in use until 1883, when a new tunic was introduced common to both regiments with the exception of the regimental buttons, six of which were on the back of the skirt. This tunic was basically of Second Life Guards pattern but with First Life Guards lace on the collar and also on all edges of the pointed cuff, the circles of russia now being on the inside of the lace of the cuff. The skirt opening was cut straight. This pattern tunic was continued after the amalgamation and is sill in use today.

The scarlet tunics worn by the Bandmasters took some time to become standardized, if indeed they ever were. Photographs show that Bandmaster Waterson, in the eighteen-sixties and seventies, wore a Troop Corporal Major's tunic. Bandmasters Englefield and Miller both wore band tunics. Bandmaster Winterbottom of the Second Regiment wore an officer's tunic in the eighteen-eighties. There is a photograph of Bandmaster Bilton of The Blues, taken just prior to the Great War, showing him wearing a Squadron Corporal Major's tunic which is the same pattern, apart from the colour, as that worn by Waterson.

The epaulettes on the tunics of Waterson and Miller were the standard type worn with aiguillettes. Winterbottom, Englefield and Bilton were wearing a slightly larger version of the musicians' plaited type. All the Bandmasters wore 1st class aiguillettes but uniquely from the right shoulder, the position which in all other cases denotes an officer rank. The aiguillettes of Warrant Officers and Non-Commissioned Officers are worn from the left shoulder and are fastened centrally by a small loop of gold russia to the bottom fastening hook of the collar. Corporals of Horse and above wear 1st class aiguillettes, Corporals 2nd class and, since the early nineteen-twenties, Lance Corporals, have worn a simple version which do not go under the arm. Originally they had a small loop of gold russia attached to the centre of the cord. This was looped over the left epaulette so that the whole of the aiguillette rested on the left breast. This method was only in use for about two years, after which the aiguillette itself was looped over the epaulette.

Life Guard Bandmasters never wore any badges of rank in any dress with one exception, Second Lieutenant Hall, who wore his officers' star. Directors of Music have always worn the tunic and aiguillettes of their rank.

Second Life Guards Band playing for Church service showing white pouches c.1895

About 1903 the trumpeters of the Second Life Guards, when on King's Guard, again wore cuirasses for a short period.

When dismounted and wearing scarlet tunics, blue overalls with double scarlet stripes, each $1\frac{1}{2}$ inches wide for the Firsts and $1\frac{1}{4}$ inches wide for the Seconds, $\frac{1}{2}$ inch apart with a scarlet welt down the centre, are worn over black wellington boots with spurs. Whitened buff waist belt and sword slings are always worn and, depending on the order, a white crossbelt with black pouch is sometimes worn. The Life Guards wear overalls of First Life Guards pattern. In 1895 the Second Life Guards Band were wearing a white music pouch, in place of the black pouch, on the crossbelt. This practice continued until at least 1912. During the eighteen-seventies they wore white music pouches on the waist belt to the right of the buckle. On the pouch was a badge similar to that on the belt buckle. When mounted, a white music pouch was worn on the sheepskin on the right front arch by both bands.

148

The Bandmasters and Directors of Music, when wearing scarlet tunics, wear a white waist belt, sword slings and carry a sword. White crossbelts are worn when ordered. On state occasions Directors of Music wear gold belts and sword slings. When a helmet is worn in these orders of dress, white gauntlets are also worn.

When conducting the Band in concerts and on parades when the Band are wearing forage caps, the Bandmasters and Directors of Music wear a blue frock coat with white waist belt, sword slings and sword, short white gloves, overalls, wellington boots, spurs and forage cap.

Up until 1882 gold lace good conduct stripes were worn, by those entitled, on the lower right sleeve of the scarlet tunic and stable jacket, by all ranks up to and including Corporal of Horse. After 1882 the stripes were worn on the lower left sleeve, but now only by Musicians, Trumpeters, Troopers and Boys.

Waist belt buckles were changed in 1882 from a Life Guards pattern common to both regiments to a Household Cavalry pattern used also by The Blues. This change was made gradually and the new buckles only issued to new recruits. Since 1882 the only change in the buckle has been the crown, in 1901 and again in 1953, although some Victorian buckles were still in use in 1965. About the same time as the change of buckle, a brass ring replaced the triangular fitting on the belt used to suspend the short sword sling.

On the re-introduction of full dress for the Band in 1949, the clothing used was pre-war stock and the number of band tunics that had survived the war and the moth was small. Consequently most of the Band had to make do with troopers' tunics until late 1952, when new band tunics were again manufactured. The troopers' tunics are easily recognizable by the gold chevrons on the cuffs.

During a visit to Singapore and Malaysia in 1967 the dress for out-of-doors engagements was overalls, wellington boots, forage cap, crossbelt and No. 3 Dress white tunic with aiguillettes where appropriate.

On 30 March, 1951, a most striking change was made to the Band full dress uniform. On Easter Sunday of that year the Band, together with the Band of the Coldstream Guards, were playing on the East Terrace of Windsor Castle watched by, among others, HM King George VI. At some time during the afternoon His Majesty sent down two messages to Major Lemoine. One was an order telling him to unhook his sword and the second was an order for the Band of The Life Guards to wear the same colour plumes as the rest of the regiment, that is to say white instead of the traditional red. On the following Tuesday the change of plumes was completed at Knightsbridge Barracks. Whether or not the Trumpeters were specifically excluded or did not change because the King only referred to the Band is not certain, but it is probable that an enquiry was made of him regarding the trumpeters. The Bandmasters and Directors of Music have generally worn white plumes, although Miller of the Firsts wore red prior to his commission, as did some of his predecessors. Another very noticeable change took place in July, 1985, when the traditional blue cape with blue stand collar was replaced by a scarlet cape, fastened by five staybrite regimental buttons, with a large blue collar identical to the cloak collar. These capes had been authorized on 12 July, 1972, and taken into store on 28 March, 1985.

The white music pouches used on mounted band were, since 1950, attached to the offside connecting strap instead of on the front arch of the sheepskin. In 1960 Captain Jackson discontinued these pouches.

The cloak worn by the Band of The Life Guards in regimental dress is identical to those of the troops, rank chevrons being worn on the lower right sleeve. The Director of Music wears the crimson officers' cloak with appropriate rank badges on the epaulettes. The other ranks' cloak is scarlet with a large blue collar. It has a small scarlet belt at the back which is only used to gather the back of the cloak in when dismounted.

In 1982 it was decided that, when the two Household Cavalry bands in regimental uniform are massed and cloaked, state cloaks should be worn. The state cloak is crimson with a dark blue velvet collar fastened by hooks and eyes, unlike the scarlet cloak which is fastened by a single row of brass or staybrite buttons. It has a strip of gold lace 2 inches wide round the collar, down both front edges and round the edges of the rear vent.

The Royal Horse Guards and latterly the Blues and Royals trumpeters, when on King's or Queen's Guard, have for many years worn the state cloak. Until 1966 their band always wore the blue regimental cloak. At this time an inspection of cloaks was suddenly sprung on the band with very little warning. On a preliminary inspection by the Trumpet Major it was evident that the moths had done a thorough job on the cloaks, which had not seen the light of day for some years. The Trumpet Major, being an old soldier, immediately had the answer. The whole band was sent to the full dress store to draw up state cloaks for the inspection. From that day The Blues, and then The Blues and Royals, have worn state cloaks whenever cloaks were ordered to be worn.

Other orders of dress include the working and stable dress, of which there have been many variations and combinations. The scarlet stable jacket with blue collar and cuffs and blue epaulettes edged with gold russia lace was in use by 1828. The First Life Guards band jacket had numerous gilt studs down the front opening, but was fastened by other means, possibly hooks and eyes. The Second's jacket was fastened by twelve brass buttons. The Trumpet Major of the Seconds had ½ inch gold lace at the top of his cuffs, round the edges of his collar and epaulettes. By 1875 there had been some changes, particularly in the Second Regiment; the previously straight blue cuff was now shaped up to a central point, with gold russia separating the blue and scarlet; narrow plaited braid epaulettes

Guard Order Egypt
1954–56, Trumpeter
G. R. Lawn

had replaced those of blue cloth. At some time before 1886 the collar of the Second's was edged with gold russia as were all the edges of the jacket. Gold russia lace with an Austrian knot at the top was sewn over the two back seams of the jacket. The russia on the cuff by now also had an Austrian knot above the point. The First Regiment were issued with new stable jackets on the Monday following 31 May, 1884, but there appears to be no noticeable difference. Again, on 23 May, 1888, First Life Guard orders said, 'New stable dress ordered'.

The trousers worn with stable dress were at one time white and then blue, followed by claret and, later, blue overalls were taken into use. Stable dress order survived until 1914.

Playing-out order for the Bands in 1830 was stable jacket, white trousers and a forage cap with no peak. The same order was in use in 1849, although sometimes the full dress coatee and peak cap were worn.

Another type of tunic worn and not part of full dress is the blue patrol tunic. This was introduced during the eighteen-nineties as a drill jacket and is made of blue serge with stand collar, epaulettes, two skirt and two breast patch pockets fastened with brass buttons and five more buttons down the front. The drill jacket originally had no pockets. Soon after its introduction the two breast pockets were added. It has generally been worn with blue overalls and forage cap. The photograph on page 148 shows the Second Life Guards Band in blue patrol jacket and overalls, wearing white crossbelt and helmet without plume. Up to 1920 the blue jacket was used as a drill tunic for rehearsals and, when worn on mounted parades, blue pantaloons with Life Guards scarlet stripes, hessian boots, forage cap and white crossbelt completed this dress. During the nineteen-thirties the jacket was usually used as a form of mess dress but since 1953, on its re-issue, the Band have worn it mainly as a comfortable relief from the scarlet tunic between performances and for travelling to and from engagements; no belts are worn on these occasions.

Head-dress has been the most varied article of working dress, generally called the forage cap; the earliest type was similar in shape to a Royal Navy Seaman's cap of today. These caps were in use by the eighteen-twenties and were blue with a scarlet band. There was also a more dressy version with a gold band. By 1851 this had progressed to a blue cap with a scarlet band and a black peak edged with ½ inch-wide gold braid. The band and trumpeters of the First Regiment wore on the cap a brass grenade badge similar to that of the Grenadier Guards. By 1895 the crown of the cap had been reduced in size and a strip of gold russia was sewn round the top of the scarlet band. A photograph of Trumpet Major W. J.

Cubis, Second Life Guards c.1865, shows gold russia on both edges of the scarlet band and an embroidered crown on the blue. Soon the cap had straight sides, the First Regiment having one strip of gold russia dividing scarlet and blue for the Trumpet Major and Band Corporal of Horse only, the braid on the peak was by now ⅜ inch wide, except for the Trumpet Major whose was ⅝ inch. The Second Regiment band and trumpeters all had gold lace round the top, bottom and centre of the wall of the cap and all Non-Commissioned Officers had in addition an embroidered crown badge. These caps were discontinued for other ranks on 7 August, 1884, when they were replaced by the pillbox. The blue pillbox with scarlet band had two strips of gold lace, one at the top of the scarlet and one at the bottom. Later, in the eighteen-nineties, a strip of gold russia was added round the top of the pillbox. An emroidered crown badge was worn by all NCOs of both bands. A pillbox without gold lace had been in use for some time before, for wearing in camp. In 1872 the First Life Guards Band were wearing glengarries at camp; some wore a small circular badge, probably unofficial. The Second Life Guards also wore the glengarry. When the glengarry was first worn or how long it lasted is not known.

In 1903 the pillbox was superseded by the pattern of forage cap still in use today. These were worn with no badge until 1920, when a brass Household Cavalry badge, which had been approved in 1913, was taken into use by both regiments. In the Life Guards the badge was worn with the crown sitting at the top of the scarlet band and the chin strap pushed behind the protruding end of the garter, so showing even strips of scarlet and blue between the chin strap and peak. Since the Second World War this had been forgotten and the strap is now usually worn resting on the peak. Corporals of Horse and above, in the bands, wear the officers' quality gilt and enamel badge, the braiding on the peak also differs from the ranks in the regiments. Originally all except the Trumpet Major and Band Corporal of Horse wore one strip of braid on the peak, the Trumpet Major and Band Corporal of Horse had two. From 1919 these two senior ranks wore three, but there is a photograph of Corporal of Horse H. Harman, believed to have been taken before 1922, wearing four. Since the late nineteen-twenties all Corporals of Horse and above in the Band wore four. About 1959 troopers took one strip into wear but no change was made to band caps until about 1970, when all Lance Corporals and Lance Corporals of Horse in the Band and Regiment took to wearing two and all band ranks of Corporal of Horse and above, except the Director of Music, took five into wear. The Director of Music wears the standard officers' forage cap. All the aforementioned forage caps, with the exception of the plain pillbox and the glengarry, have been part of walking out dress.

Khaki clothing, which has over the years been of many shades and materials, was first worn by Life Guards in 1882 during the campaign in Egypt. The head-dress worn in 1882 and also for the Boer War of 1899 was the Wolseley helmet.

The introduction of khaki service dress in August, 1913, saw the Bands and trumpeters looking unusually drab. The articles of dress were the jacket with a stand and fall collar; brass buttons were of regimental pattern and brass shoulder titles L.G., with either 1 or 2 above, were worn. The 2nd Life Guards wore a white lanyard on the right shoulder. In 1882 and also the Boer and First World War Squadron Trumpeters of the 2nd Life Guards wore embroidered worsted crossed trumpets on the upper right sleeve of their khaki jackets. Trousers were worn on dismounted occasions, pantaloons, puttees and spurs when mounted or when ordered on some dismounted occasions. The service dress peaked cap with brown leather chin strap was the head-dress. The newly introduced regimental cap badges were worn on this cap. The Director of Music's service dress cap is the unique Life Guards officers' pattern which has a brown leather band round the edge of the peak. The regimental cap badges for both regiments were issued bronzed, but almost immediately the Second Life Guards polished theirs. The polished brass badge continued after the amalgamation. For the Guards' march through London in 1919 white crossbelts were added to the mounted service dress. The greatcoat issued with the service dress was, and is, the British Warm, worn in the Life Guards with the top button unfastened, The Blues fastening theirs to the top.

Between the wars service dress for parades became a little more colourful, with the addition of white crossbelt, white sword slings worn from under the jacket, white buckskin gloves for trumpeters, and the red and blue forage cap. The grips on the pantaloons were blancoed with cobra blanco which was a sandy yellow with a light brown tint. Since 1939 sword slings have not been worn. From its introduction until 1943 and from 1952 until 1962, basic service dress was the everyday wear for the Band.

The trumpeters in Palestine in 1940 wore mounted service dress shirt-sleeve order, with bandolier in place of the white crossbelt and the addition of a brown leather waist belt. The bandolier had been worn prior to the First World War when on manoeuvrres in blue tunics and was continued with service dress for manoeuvrres and morning exercise until the abolition of service dress in 1962. The head-dress was the topi with a puggaree which had a narrow strip of scarlet and blue around the top for these, the last Life Guards to serve abroad as a mounted unit.

During 1943 the Band were issued with battledress on which was the regimental shoulder flash of The Life Guards embroidered in royal blue on red, the headdress was either the service dress cap or dark blue beret. Web belts and anklets (gaiters), blancoed cobra, were also worn. The British Warm greatcoat, although a cavalry item, continued to be worn with battledress by the Band, while the Regiment wore the long infantry greatcoat.

Service dress was re-introduced for the Band soon after the Second World War, although, until moving to Knightsbridge in 1952, battledress continued as everyday wear. Life Guards musicians attending courses at Kneller Hall were still wearing battledress in 1955, with the embellishment of Kneller Hall company flashes on their shoulder straps and, in some cases, good conduct stripes whitened, as was done in the Royal Artillery if the Company Commander happened to be a Gunner. Their web belts were blancoed green.

The trumpeters with the Regiment in the Suez Canal Zone of Egypt, 1954–56, were dressed as follows:

Day Guard Order for the Duty Trumpeter

Khaki drill jacket tucked into khaki drill shorts, the sleeves of the jacket rolled up above the elbow, black ankle boots, khaki woollen hose tops, cobra blancoed web waist belt and anklets. The brass buckles on the anklets were altered to provide a tighter fit. From the middle of 1955 khaki drill shirts could be used instead of jackets. The headdress was the forage cap.

## Night Guard Order

Khaki drill jacket, with sleeves unrolled, tucked into khaki drill trousers, black ankle boots, web belt and forage cap.

Night Guard Cold Weather
As above with the addition of a khaki woollen pullover worn over the jacket and outside the trousers, the web belt over the pullover.

## Winter Guard Order

Battledress with black ankle boots, web belt, anklets and forage cap.

Working dress was as for Day Guard Order but with either blue beret or service dress cap, a regimental stable belt was permitted to replace the web belt.

The Regiment's next trip abroad was to Aden, where the trumpeters' dress was much the same as for the Canal Zone, the exceptions were the whitened buff full dress waist belt, anklets blancoed white and regimental hose tops of blue with dark red turnover.

About 1960 new stand-up stiff collars replaced the stand and fall type on the service dress which had been in use since 1913 and in 1962 black knee boots replaced puttees. For a few months in the late fifties or early sixties London District flashes were worn by the Band on the upper sleeves of service dress.

Cyprus, 1964, saw three trumpeters of The Life Guards, J. Barnbrook R. White and Lance Corporal D. T. McQueen become the first musicians of the British Army to wear the blue beret of the United Nations.

The introduction of No. 2 dress to supersede service dress took place in 1962 and The Life Guards Band were one of the first units to be issued with this new 'American style' clothing. Brass L.G. shoulder titles were on the shoulder straps until 31 October, 1989, when they were replaced by the red and blue regimental titles previously worn on battledress. Everyday working dress from 1962 was No. 2 dress with forage cap. This continued until 1969 when the Household Cavalry Bands followed the long-established custom of the Foot Guards Bands by wearing civilian clothes for normal rehearsal days. At the present time, if required to wear uniform in barracks, barrack dress is worn. This consists of: in summer, shirt sleeve order of open neck khaki shirt, green barrack dress trousers, black shoes, regimental stable belt and forage cap. Other times, khaki shirt and tie, green barrack dress trousers, khaki pullover, black shoes, regimental stable belt worn outside the pullover, and forage cap. Since 1978, when on exercise as medical assistants, combat dress is worn.

## Instrument slings and aprons

Carrying slings for dismounted drummers were originally whitened buff, while those for basses were black leather. Since c.1920 standard pattern slings, common to all Guards Bands, have been in use. These are dark blue, edged with scarlet piping, with gold lace down either side for drums and basses and a single strip of lace on the saxophone slings. When in khaki, brown leather slings are used.

Until the mid-nineteen-fifties, the bass drummer and side drummers wore white buckskin aprons; since that time scarlet cloth aprons have been used by the bass drummer, cymbal player, basses, euphoniums and saxophones.

## Sheepskins and beards

Prior to 1865, both Life Guards Bands used white sheepskins edged with scalloped blue cloth. In 1865 the First Life Guards changed to black. There are paintings showing the First Life Guards Band with black sheekpskins edged with scalloped scarlet cloth. Since the amalgamation The Life Guards Band and Trumpeters have used black sheepskins. Trumpeters' horses of The Life Guards wear a red and black mixed beard, thereby continuing the custom of the First Life Guards. Those of the Second Life Guards did not wear beards.

Order of Dress for Trooping The Colour rehearsal, 1950s

# CHAPTER 16

# Band Aid (1978-94)

Orders for 2 October, 1978, required the Band to report on that day for medical training, which was to last a week and eventually became an annual event. This week was the beginning of the first major change in the role of the Band since the formation of its predecessors, the Bands of the First and Second Life Guards, almost two hundred years previously. Members of the Regiment stared in disbelief at the sight of badly wounded musicians being tended by their colleagues in the car park adjoining the band block. The troopers' disbelief was surpassed by that of the musicians, whose real wounds were the shocks to the system caused by this sudden warlike activity which interrupted the traditional daily routine that had remained the same for almost a century. After completing their training the musicians were qualified as Medical Assistants class 3.

Earlier in the year the Band had received two reports on its efficiency. After the Kneller Hall inspection they were classified as 'outstanding', while the Silver Stick's report on mounted bands said, 'The Life Guards were excellent and The Blues and Royals not up to standard.'

After some years absence the Shrewsbury Flower Show was on the Band calendar for 1978. Another KAPE tour was successfully negotiated, this time in the Manchester area where the Band returned later in the year for the Manchester Tattoo. 1978 had more than the usual number of film premieres at which either the Band or Trumpeters performed, these included 'Revenge of the Pink Panther' and 'Star Wars'. Among the new engagements was the opening concert of the Brighton Festival given together with the Band of the Coldstream Guards. Three more tattoos in which The Life Guards Band took part were at Plymouth, Wembley and Berlin.

Shortly before leaving for Berlin, a call from the Silver Stick ordered the Band to provide six trumpeters for a tattoo in Iran which coincided with the Berlin Tattoo, their places in the band for Berlin being taken by trumpeters from The Blues and Royals. After rehearsing at South Cerney, Gloucestershire, the six Iran-bound trumpeters left RAF Brize Norton aboard a Boeing 707 of the Iranian Air Force. Accommodation in Iran was the Asian Olympic Village, fourteen miles from Tehran, which at first view appeared quite reasonable. The trumpeters were soon to discover otherwise, as their self-contained flats had no cookers and water was heated by a smelly paraffin-fuelled boiler situated next to the 'hole-in-the-floor' lavatory. The tattoo, which included the bands of the King's Own Scottish Borderers, Royal Green Jackets and two bands of the Royal Marines, played at Esfahan (Iran's second city), Ahwaz, Shiraz and Tabriz. The final week was spent in Tehran performing at a variety of functions which included a show at the British Embassy and playing before a football match between the Iranian 'B' Team and Manchester United, who won the match 1–0.

The Colonel of the Regiment, Admiral of the Fleet Earl Mountbatten, known in his regiment as Colonel Dickie, was murdered on 27 August, 1979. The Band marched massed with the Band of The Blues and Royals in the funeral procession. Even on such a solemn occasion as the rehearsal for the funeral the opportunity of confusing a Foot Guard Sergeant Major could not be missed. Each section of the procession was kept in position by a Sergeant Major of the Foot Guards in the capacity of parade marshal. At one point the Household Cavalry band had quickened its pace and was too far ahead of its correct position. The marshal for the band shouted out, 'Corporal Major, call out the time,' which received the reply from Corporal of Horse Charlie Jolley, 'Ten past eight'.

After a visit to the Regiment in Cyprus for a United Nations Medal presentation parade, the Band were once again mounted for the Wembley Pageant. In June, 1979, Corporal of Horse Robert Ely was appointed Bandmaster of the 2nd Battalion, The Parachute Regiment.

Lance Corporal of Horse Peter Watts was awarded a certificate by The Society for the Protection of Life from Fire in testimony of distinguished conduct while engaged in the rescue of life from fire when he rescued a traffic accident victim on 12 July, 1981.

The Band played for the fireworks display in Hyde Park as part of the celebrations of the wedding of HRH Prince Charles to Lady Diana Spencer on 29 July, 1981. During this year Germany was visited twice, the first occasion was with the horses for the Berlin Tattoo and then, on 15 December, to Detmold to visit the Regiment, during which one of the more pleasing engagements was a Christmas concert for German OAPs.

In May, 1982, Corporal of Horse G. W. C. Jarvis was appointed Bandmaster of the Queen's Own Highlanders and was later commissioned into that regiment. Less than a year later Corporal of Horse R. Owen followed him into the ranks of bandmasters when in March, 1983, he was appointed Bandmaster of the Queen's Lancashire Regiment. Five years later he was Bandmaster of the Junior School of Music, Bovington, and in 1989 became School Bandmaster at Kneller Hall. He was commissioned a Captain and appointed Director of Music Infantry South in 1992 and first Director of Music of the Light Division Band in 1994.

The first opportunity of putting their medical training into practice, for which they had been trained annually since 1978, came on 22 September, 1982, when the Band were put on standby for a TUC day of action. The ambulances, manned by musicians of The Life Guards, were on standby at various police stations around the capital but the official policy was that they were not to be used. One ambulance was, however, called out in an emergency on the authority of the police, to a heart-attack victim whose life was saved by the ambulance crew of Lance Corporals David Bole and Paul Morton. This action was reported extensively in the national newspapers.

Spain was visited by Life Guards trumpeters for the first time since the Peninsular War when, in September, Trumpet Major Morris and three trumpeters went to Jerez as part of the British contingent for the 1983 vintage sherry celebrations. The Trumpet Major's verdict on the trip was: 'The best I ever did,' and his appreciation of sherry, especially when free, had reached new heights.

Band Corporal Major R. J. (Percy) Fletcher retired in December, 1983, and his successor F. J. Harman, the youngest band Warrant Officer in the British Army, had, early in the New Year, to prepare the Band for its Kneller Hall inspection as Major Richards was confined to bed with a severe spinal ailment. At the time of the inspection the Director of Music was still incapacitated and the resulting 'Excellent' grading was much to the credit of the new Band Corporal Major and also the Director of Music, who had left his band in fine order. Another retirement of note in 1983 was Trumpet Major A. E. Close, who had first retired in 1977 to become a publican but had rejoined in 1978. Tony Close was the only person to hold the appointment of Trumpet Major of The Life Guards twice.

The new year of 1984 began with the retirement, in January, of the Director of Music, Major Richards, after thirteen and a half years in The Life Guards. The new Director, Captain J. G. McColl's first taste of band work with The Life Guards was a brisk early morning parade at the Guards Depot. After four years at Knightsbridge the Band moved to Windsor in February, suffering the loss on the way of a box of cornet solos.

The main event of 1984 was Exercise Lionheart, which was held in Germany. Preparation for this started in the first week of September at Woolwich, where the Band teamed up with 30 General Hospital to learn their role for Lionheart and being instructed in the finer points of lighting a Tilley lamp or, in Army terms, lamp, wickless, kerosene, for the use of. The initial role of the Band was to help set up and run a rear combat zone hospital, based at the British Military Hospital at Iserlohn. 12 September found the Band in full combat kit looking like fighting soldiers. After spending a night in a hangar at RAF Wildenrath their first few days were spent practising what had been learnt at Woolwich.

During the exercise proper, which lasted a week, the musicians acted as stretcher bearers and usually worked a twelve-hour day. The Director of Music, meantime, was acting as one of the General Duty Officers, working in the Command Post. His main task was to ensure enough tea and coffee was available for the 'workers'. This was in addition to any other task that was either too technical or too dirty for the 'real' doctors to bother with. This included the siting and connection of generators for all the wards as stand-bys in case of bombing. He also helped in putting together an internal telephone network, which apparently almost worked. Most of the Director's time, however, was spent as an interpreter dealing with the German civil labour.

On the final muster parade the Band were told to remain behind: a little extra praise perhaps, but no, they were informed that they were to go to Ostend to offload two hospital trains and then load the casualties on to Hercules aircraft. This period of intense activity did not end on their arrival back in the UK, for, after a whole day off, they were immediately despatched to Newmarket to prepare for a midnight mounted band display.

One engagement of historical significance was the El Alamein reunion at Blackpool, attended by Herr Manfred Rommel and Viscount Montgomery, the sons of the El Alamein protagonists. The choice of the Band of The Life Guards to perform at this function was particularly appropriate in view of its wartime nickname 'Monty's Pets'.

One day, in the early part of 1985, The Life Guards Band, with that of the Welsh Guards, paraded at Wellington Barracks in the morning to rehearse dismounted in formations of various sizes and combinations. In the afternoon the perfected spectacle of two gradually diminishing bands was paraded for the benefit of some bowler-hatted gentlemen from Whitehall. Later in the year the outcome of the day was the reduction of the establishment of the Band once again, this time to 36. Until December, 1960, the authorized establishment had been a total of 49. Since that date frequent changes were made as shown below.

| Date | DoM | Wo2 | SCpl | CoH | LCoH | LCpl | Musn | Total |
|---|---|---|---|---|---|---|---|---|
| 23 Dec 60 | 1 | 0 | 0 | 4* | 4 | 4 | 32 | 45 |
| 14 Jul 67 | 1 | 0 | 0 | 4* | 4 | 4 | 31 | 44 |
| 01 Apr 71 | 1 | 2 | 2 | 5 | 6 | 6 | 22 | 44 |
| 01 Apr 80 | 1 | 2 | 2 | 5 | 6 | 6 | 20 | 42 |
| 01 Apr 81 | 1 | 2 | 2 | 4 | 7 | 7 | 17 | 40 |
| 01 Apr 85 | 1 | 2 | 2 | 4 | 6 | 6 | 15 | 36 |
| 01 Jul 89 | 1 | 2 | 2 | 4 | 6 | 6 | 14 | 35 |
| Options for Ch | 1 | 2 | 2 | 4 | 5 | 7 | 14 | 35 |

\* One to be Band CoH/Trumpet Major on time promotion in the rank of SQMC/S. Cpl.
One WO2 was cut in '81 but given back later.
Options for Change row is provisional.

From 1985 the Band were no longer required to provide trumpeters for the Mounted Squadron, volunteer troopers from the Squadron being trained as trumpeters for this duty. They are not appointed Trumpeter and so retain the rank and title of Trooper.

Ironically, for the 36 musicians remaining, 1985 was very busy. In a sixteen-day period in June, seventeen engagements were carried out. This year was the twentieth anniversary of the granting of the Freedom of the

Leading The Queen's Life Guard to Whitehall 1993

Knightsbridge, January 1995

*Back Row*  L/CoH PC Wilman, MUS D.R.M. Carter,
MUS D.L.Isherwood, CoH P.D. Lazenbury, MUS D.A. Smart,
L/CPL N.L. Maher, CoH O.N. Gook, S/CPL J. Woodhouse,
MUS I.R. Sturgeon, L/CoH R.M. Allen, MUS J. Field

*Centre Row*  MUS N. D. Bowen, L/CoH D. M. Bole, CoH N. A. White,
L/CPL K. A. Pearson, MUS D. J. Taylor, MUS A. K. Walsh,
L/CPL I. J. Stott, MUS M. D. Walters, MUS M. P. Whybrow

*Front Row*  T/M P. J. Carson, MUS I. G. Corney, MUS N. G. Riseley,
L/CPL N. J. Goodchild, BCM I. Graves, L/CPL J. Matthews,
MUS P. D'Arcy, Maj. C. J. Reeves, SQMC R. M. Young,
L/CoH B. J. Dutton, MUS V. T. Hinchliffe,
L/CPL G. W. Wheeler

Royal Borough of New Windsor and, on 13 April, the two regiments of Household Cavalry exercised their privilege by riding through Windsor led by the massed mounted bands. Four days after this event there was a State Visit, in Windsor, by the Life President of Malawi. The street liners on this occasion were found by The Life Guards. The Band marched the Regiment to their positions, dressed, as were the Regiment, in khaki No. 2 Dress, a most unusual dress for The Life Guards Band on a ceremonial occasion.

One chore the Band had not, for many years, had to perform was playing for the officers in their mess. On 1 October they came close when they were required to play on the lawn of the Officers' House during a cocktail party. This had come about after the Director of Music had found that the Officers' Lawn was the only available space to rehearse a marching display. This spectacle was seen by the Commanding Officer who, with great vision, could see the Band performing there for his cocktail party.

All the routine military and civil engagements of recent years continued throughout 1985 and '86 with few additions. One addition, however, came about in 1986 through the eagle eyes of an Australian journalist who, reading the press release for a forthcoming tour of Australia by the Scots Guards Band, noticed that the son of that band's Director of Music was a trumpeter in The Life Guards Band. Shortly afterwards Musician Carson and three trumpet-playing colleagues were on their way to Australia to accompany Major Carson and the Scots Guards Band on their tour.

A telephone call at the end of May, 1987, to the Band Office from Rosehaugh Stanhope Development plc enquired if the Band would be interested in going to Tokyo on 11 July, which coincided with the last day of a week on Pine Walk bandstand, Bournemouth, for which contracts had already been signed. Another band was soon found to deputise on 11 July and The Life Guards Band duly took off from Heathrow, arriving in Tokyo on Sunday the 12th. By 7.30 that evening a recce by the Band for the following day's engagements had been carried out and they were back to the sumptious luxury of the Hotel Ana for some much-needed rest before cramming a week's engagements into the next day, the itinery of which was:

| | |
|---|---|
| 0530 | Breakfast |
| 0600 | Depart for TV Station |
| 0630 | Rehearse for TV morning show |

| | |
|---|---|
| 0745 | Live performance on TV |
| 0830 | Depart TV Station |
| 0930 | Arrive Mitsokoshi department store (Tokyo's Harrods) |
| 1000 | Rehearse march through store |
| 1100 | March into store and concert |
| 1145 | March out of store |
| 1150 | Depart store for Hibiya Park |
| 1210 | Arrive at Park |
| 1230 | March through Park to concert location |
| 1245 | Concert |
| 1330 | Shopping! |
| 1430 | Depart for Hotel Okura |
| 1500 | Rehearse for presentation |
| 1645 | Presentation – including Brass Quintet |
| 2030 | Trumpeters and Marching Band |
| 2100 | The rest of the day is free! |

Early on Tuesday the 14th the Band left Tokyo on a direct flight to Heathrow, arriving that evening. The following morning the Great Yorkshire Show was the contrasting destination for a weary band of travelling musicians.

One band axed in the cuts of 1985 was that of the Royal Military Academy, Sandhurst, who obviously still needed a band. The solution to this was for the remaining Army bands each to take their turn as the Academy Band. The Life Guards' turn came in 1987, when they were at Sandhurst from 7 September to 11 December.

During another routine visit to The Life Guards Squadron in Cyprus in April, 1988, concerts were given for various foreign contingents which included the Austrians and Canadians. The Canadian connection was continued the following month when the Band accompanied the Royal Canadian Mounted Police Musical Ride at the Royal Windsor Horse Show. For their performances the Band was conducted by a Sergeant from the Mounties Band in Ottawa. B. C. M. Fred Harman left the Army on 31 December, 1988, after twenty-four years' service and was followed into civilian life shortly afterwards by Staff Corporal David Mean, the Band's solo clarinetist.

Early in 1989 the Band failed their Kneller Hall inspection at Windsor. On 21 March they were subjected to another inspection, this time the result was an excellent grading. Some members of the Band commented that there was no difference between their performances during the two inspections.

In 1989 it was decreed that the Household Cavalry Bands should each have a civilian secretary. On 5 May, 1989, a civil servant, Mr Keith Whitworth, a former bassoonist, took up the position which by a strange coincidence he had held from 1975 to 1987, finishing in the rank of W.O.II. There had only been a permanent band secretary since about 1946, the first of whom was Corporal Tony Monaghan, a pianist. On his demob in 1956, Corporal Ian D. Gunn, a tenor sax player replaced him and remained until 1972, leaving in the rank of Staff Corporal. Two secretaries followed in quick succession, cornet player Lance Corporal of Horse Malcolm Rose from 1972 to 1974 and then W.O.II Brian J. Frost from 1974 to 1975. Frost was later solo clarinet and Band Corporal Major. The period between Whitworth's two terms was filled by Lance Corporal David Bole, a euphonium player.

In September, 1989, Major Gerry McColl resigned as Director of Music and was replaced by Captain Colin Reeves from the Alanbrooke Band of the Royal Artillery.

A national ambulance strike saw the Band widely dispersed throughout Greater London from 8 November, 1989, until March, 1990, on Operation Orderly, manning ambulances once more. Their stations were as far apart as Banstead and Whetstone. A week off from their medical duties in January was a welcome relief but during this week the move from Windsor to Knightsbridge was completed.

Before the end of Operation Orderly four trumpeters escaped and fitted in a trip to Detroit for the North American Motor Show. The trumpeters were back in the States in May, this time in Salt Lake City for the 50th anniversary celebrations of the Utah Symphony Orchestra. In March the Director of Music had been welcomed back to the Band having completed and survived his riding course. He immediately set about the task of preparing the Band for its usual summer season, which turned out to be much shortened due to events beyond his control.

The Iraqi invasion of Kuwait on 2 August, 1990, brought about the possibility of military intervention by Britain and some other nations. By November plans for action had been drawn up. The Life Guards' Band part in what was code-named Operation Granby began on 12 November with a move to South Cerney for five days' special medical training with 16 Field Ambulance Group. While there they were also called upon to fit out new vehicles in readiness for the expected casualties. On the 26th they travelled to Germany to visit the Regiment to find, on their arrival, that most of the Regiment had left to play their part in the Gulf War. Returning to Knightsbridge on Thursday, 6 December the Band were, on the following Monday, moved to Bulford for more training, some of which was at a small camp later used to detain Iraq nationals. The latter part of the ten-day period was taken up by exercises between Brize Norton and Aldershot or Woolwich Military Hospitals. Time was also found for rehearsals and for the Major General's inspection at Windsor of The Blues and Royals, plus the Household Cavalry Mounted Regiment's carol concert and brick-hanging ceremony. After three weeks leave over Christmas and the New Year and with the Allied Troops already in the Gulf region, the Band were deployed firstly at Aldershot, then RAF Manston in Kent, where their duties were mainly meeting flights at Gatwick and RAF Northolt to convey casualties to hospital at Woolwich. This continued through February until stand down from Operation Granby eventually came on 1 March, 1991. The final act for the Band was handing over their vehicles at Bulford.

In July, 1991, the Government announced the future union of The Life Guards and Blues and Royals. From this time there was much speculation as to the future of the bands of the two regiments. Rumours were plentiful and included the amalgamation of the two bands. The union of the two regiments took place at Windsor on 19 October, 1992, and on Budget Day November, 1993, the announcement concerning service bands was made and, much to the relief of the Household Cavalry Bands, they were to remain separate. The Life Guards Band at this time was over-strength and two members accepted voluntary redundancy which took effect in October, 1994. Also part of Options for Change or 'What do we do with the Bandmasters' was the decree that each band should have a W.O.I Bandmaster as assistant or deputy to the Director of Music. He would also, at other times, play in the band. Tim Cooper, an oboe player, was appointed Bandmaster, The Life Guards, on 31 March, 1994.

1992, 1993 and 1994 saw the life of the Band carry on as usual, with all the regular engagements and military duties, such as the annual firing on the ranges at Pirbright, joined by the odd new venture. One such venture was on 1 April, 1993, when they travelled to Sennybridge in Wales for a passing-out parade of Oxford University OTC. In January, 1993, four trumpeters had visited the United States for five days on what, by now, had become almost a commonplace excursion. A day excursion to the Palace of Versailles was undertaken by the Band on 27 August, 1994, with a hurried return to England to take part in the Household Cavalry Mounted Regiment's open day at Bodney Camp in Norfolk the following day. Two days later Lance Corporal G. W. Wheeler left Windsor for Bosnia as Squadron Trumpeter of B Squadron, the sole representative of the Band in that troubled area.

The band's final duty of 1994 was a visit to Bosnia, which began on 17 December, when the Director of Music and twenty-five members of the band left RAF Lyneham in a Hercules aircraft bound for Split, Croatia. After a night spent attempting to sleep in a Royal Navy hangar in Split, B Squadron was visited briefly at Gorni Vakuf, Bosnia, before arriving at Vitez to entertain the Royal Highland Fusiliers. On Monday the 19th a concert for HQ Squadron at Zepce was followed by an evening concert for the regimental hierarchy and VIPs in the comparative luxury of an hotel.

The final full day began with a morning concert, at Prozor, for the Royal Gloucester, Berkshire and Wiltshire Regiment, in freezing conditions in a concert hall minus some walls. This was followed by a fleeting visit to D Squadron, The Blues and Royals, amid the shelling, at Maglaj, and finally a concert for B Squadron, The Life Guards, back at Gorni Vakuf. The flight home, on the 21st was in a VC10, destination RAF Brize Norton.

With the next move to Windsor scheduled for 1995 and the Band's diary showing many engagements for that year already booked, the temporary cessation of recruiting should, by then, be at its end and more musicians will again be joining the Band, thereby helping to continue its existence into the twenty-first century.

The Army being more professional than ever before, extraordinary happenings caused by people of character are now much less frequent. For sheer cheek the extraordinary happening on the 1959 Trooping the Colour takes some beating. A cornet player in the front rank, during Her Majesty's inspection of the Band, produced a camera from his jackboot and snapped The Queen as she rode past. The player concerned had just developed an interest in photography and decided to reverse proceedings and took photographs of the crowd as he rode from the Palace up The Mall to Horse Guards Parade. His action on Horse Guards was seen by one of the Band Corporals of Horse who reported the matter to the Trumpet Major. The Trumpet Major's reaction was that this could possibly be a court martial offence which would require the presence of the Trumpet Major. As the Trumpet Major's retirement from the Band was imminent, he did not wish to be held back so the matter was dropped.

Only a characterless government could amalgamate or disband a band that has had through its ranks such characters and musicians as have The

Life Guards during the last 334 years. With the government of the day wielding its axe on service bands at ever more frequent intervals, all who covet tradition, pomp and military music must hope that the protection prayed for in The Life Guards' collect will deflect the government axe and ensure that for many years to come, all will have the opportunity of the pleasure of hearing the Kettledrummers, Trumpeters and Band of Her Majesty's Life Guards.

## REGIMENTAL COLLECT OF THE LIFE GUARDS

*O everlasting God, King of Kings, in whose service we put on the breastplate of faith and love, and for an helmet the hope of salvation, grant we beseech Thee that The Life Guards may be faithful unto death, and receive at last the crown of life from Jesus Christ our Lord. Amen.*

# APPENDIX I

# Band Formations

The formations of the bands for dismounted parades changed many times over the years, mostly at the discretion of the Bandmaster or Director of Music. The most distinctive difference between the First and Second Regiments was that the First Regiment used one Corporal of Horse or Corporal Major from their regiment to lead the Band, while the Second Regiment used two, possibly an allusion to the two drum horse coverers employed when mounted. Another noticeable difference was the circular bass tubas of the Firsts.

## EXAMPLES

2nd Life Guards c1885

| | | | | | | | | |
|---|---|---|---|---|---|---|---|---|
| Bass | Euph | Horn | Bass | Euph | Euph | Trom | Trom | B.Trom |
| Horn | Horn | Corn | Corn | Corn | Corn | Corn | Corn | Corn |
| Clart | Clart | Clart | Clart | B.Clart | Clart | Clart | Bsn | Bsn |
| Oboe | Picc | EbClart | | | | Clart | Clart | Clart |
| | | | S.D. | B.D. | Cymb | | B.M. | |

2nd Life Guards c1914

| | | | | | | |
|---|---|---|---|---|---|---|
| Bass | Bass | Euph | Trom | Trom | B.Trom | Bass |
| Euph | T.Horn | Corn | Corn | Corn | Corn | Corn |
| S.D. | | B.D. | | Cymb | | B.M. |
| Horn | Clart | Clart | Clart | Clart | Bsn | Bsn |
| EbClart | Picc | Oboe | Clart | Clart | Clart | Clart |

1st Life Guards. Guards March through London 1919

| | | | | | | | |
|---|---|---|---|---|---|---|---|
| C.Bass | Bass | B.Trom | Trom | Trom | Bass | C.Bass | |
| Corn | Trpt | Trpt | Trpt | Trpt | Trpt | Trpt | DofM |
| Corn | Corn | Oboe | Euph | T.Horn | T.Horn | T.Horn | |
| S.D. | | | B.D. | | | Cymb | |
| Clart | Clart | Clart | T.Sax | A.Sax | T.Horn | Euph | |
| Clart | Clart | Clart | Clart | EbClart | Picc | Picc | |

## The Life Guards c1950

| | | | | | |
|---|---|---|---|---|---|
| Bass | Bass | Euph | Bass | Bass | |
| Trom | B.Trom | Euph | Trom | Trom | |
| Corn | Corn | Corn | Corn | Corn | |
| S.D. | S.D. | B.D. | | Cymb | DofM |
| Horn | Corn | Horn | Corn | Horn | |
| A.Sax | T.Sax | Clart | Bsn | Bsn | |
| Clart | Clart | Clart | Clart | Clart | |
| Clart | Clart | Clart | EbClart | Picc | |

## The Life Guards. Garter Ceremony 1964

| | | | | |
|---|---|---|---|---|
| B.Trom | Trom | Trom | Trom | B.Trom |
| Corn | Corn | Corn | Corn | Corn |
| Bass | Euph | Euph | Euph | Bass |
| Horn | Corn | Horn | Corn | Horn |
| S.D. | Clart | B.D. | Cymb | DofM |
| T.Sax | S.Sax | Clart | T.Sax | A.Sax |
| Picc | EbClart | Clart | Clart | Clart |
| Clart | Clart | Clart | Clart | Clart |

## The Life Guards. Cavalry Memorial Parade 1994

| | | B.C.M. | | |
|---|---|---|---|---|
| Trom | Trom | B.Trom | Trom | Trom |
| Bass | Bass | Euph | Bass | Bass |
| Corn | Corn | Corn | Corn | Corn |
| S.D. | DofM | B.D. | Cym | S.D. |
| Corn | Horn | | Horn | Euph |
| A.Sax | T.Sax | T.Sax | Clart | Picc |
| Clart | Clart | Clart | Clart | Clart |

Since 1983 the Band of The Life Guards, on dismounted parades, has been led by the Band Corporal Major.

The formation of the bands when mounted has not changed drastically but, like all bands, are dependent on the make-up of the band and availability of musicians. Until the latter part of the nineteenth century the mounted bands were usually composed of brass and kettledrums. Before the Second World War valve trombones were, at some period, used when the band was mounted. In the mid-nineteen-fifties a complete set of valve trombones were, on the orders of Colonel Lemoine, thrown away. In the early nineteen-sixties cornets formed the front rank of The Life Guards Band for a short period. French horns are not used on mounted band, tenor horns being used in their stead. Tenor horns were frequently used for dismounted parades prior to the First World War, the last occasion one was used was on the Freedom of Windsor Parade in May, 1965. During Major Jackson's Directorship, all except four clarinet players used saxophones on some occasions when mounted.

Grey horses, in recent years, have generally formed the rear rank. In earlier times they had formed the front rank and earlier still took whichever position the instrument of their riders dictated.

## EXAMPLES

1st Life Guards 1915

|        |        | B.M.    |       |         |
|        |        | K.D.    |       |         |
| C.Bass | Euph   | Euph    | Bass  | C.Bass  |
| Clart  | Corn   | Trom    | Trom  | B.Trom  |
| Corn   | Corn   | Corn    | Corn  | Corn    |
| Euph   | T.Horn | T.Horn  | T.Horn| T.Horn  |
| Clart  | Clart  | Clart   | Clart | Clart   |

The Life Guards c1950

|        |        | D of M |        |        |
|        |        | K.D.   |        |        |
| Bass   | Bass   | Euph   | Bass   |
| B.Trom | Trom   | Trom   | Trom   |
| Euph   | Trom   | T.Horn | T.Horn |
| Corn   | Corn   | T.Horn | Corn   |
| Corn   | Corn   | Corn   | Corn   |
| Clart  | A.Sax  | A.Sax  | T.Sax  |
| Clart  | Clart  | Clart  | Clart  |
| Clart  | Clart  | Clart  | Picc   |

The Life Guards. Trooping The Colour 1961

D of M

| K.D. (R.H.G.) | | | | K.D. | |
| Bass   | Bass   | Euph   | T.Horn | Bass  | Bass  |
| Corn   | Corn   | B.Trom | Euph   | Trom  | Trom  |
| Corn   | Corn   | Corn   | Corn   | Corn  | Corn  |
| T.Horn | T.Horn | T.Horn | T.Sax  | A.Sax | T.Sax |
| Clart  | Clart  | Picc   | Picc   | Clart | Clart |
| Clart  | Clart  | Clart  | Clart  | Clart | Clart |

The Life Guards. Trooping The Colour 1994
Massed with Blues and Royals
D of M
K.D.

| Bass | Euph | Euph | Bass |
|------|------|--------|------|
| Trom | Trom | B. Trom | Trom |
| Corn | Corn | Corn | Corn |
| Corn | T.Horn | T.Horn | Corn |
| T.Sax | A.Sax | A.Sax | Picc |
| Clart | Clart | Clart | Clart |

On occasions such as Beating Retreat on Horse Guards Parade, four trumpeters are added and ride immediately behind the kettledrummer.

Abbreviations

| A.Sax | Alto Saxophone | D of M | Director of Music |
|-------|----------------|--------|-------------------|
| B.C.M. | Band Corporal Major | EbClart | Eb Clarinet |
| B.M. | Bandmaster | Euph | Euphonium |
| Bass | Bass Tuba | Horn | French Horn |
| B.Clart | Bass Clarinet | K.D. | Kettledrums |
| B.D. | Bass Drum | Picc | Piccolo |
| Bsn | Bassoon | S.D. | Side Drum |
| B.Trom | Bass Trombone | S.Sax | Soprano Saxophone |
| C.Bass | Circular Bass Tuba | T.Horn | Tenor Horn |
| Clart | Bb Clarinet | Trom | Tenor Trombone |
| Corn | Cornet | Trpt | Trumpet |
| Cymb | Cymbals | | |

# Trumpet Majors and
# Band Corporals Major

The first Trumpet Major in the Life Guards was appointed in 1799, probably as a result of the change in status of the trumpeters made that year by enlisting them as attested soldiers and therefore being no longer under the authority of the Sergeant Trumpeter of the Royal Household. For many years in the nineteenth and early twentieth centuries the Trumpet Major's official designation was Corporal Trumpeter and then Corporal of Horse Trumpeter, not to be confused with the assistant to the Trumpet Major known as the Trumpet Corporal.

*Trumpet Majors of the First Life Guards*

|  | Appointed | Until |
|---|---|---|
| A. Lacy | 25 Sept 1810 | died 24 Jan 1812 |
| T. Harley | Jan 1812 | 6 Mar 1812 |
| J. Lieber | 7 Mar 1812 | 12 Oct 1814 |
| J. Vanderwalker | Oct 1814 | Apr 1822 |
| J. Rathbone | 30 Apr 1822 | 27 Mar 1843 |
| W. Winterbottom | 12 Apr 1843 | 23 Jul 1853 |
| T. Addey | 24 Jul 1853 | 8 Apr 1863 |
| W. Binnie | 22 Apr 1863 | 22 Jan 1869 |
| J. Raugh | 23 Jan 1869 | 8 Mar 1876 |
| J. Tully | 22 Mar 1876 | 21 Jun 1882 |
| J. Donoghue | 30 Jun 1882 | 30 Sep 1890 |
| T. Golding | 1 Oct 1890 | 1 Dec 1891 |
| W. Mayne | 19 Dec 1891 | 30 Jul 1892 |
| J. C. Barber | 1 Aug 1892 | 27 Jan 1902 |
| J. Carter | 28 Jan 1902 | 30 Apr 1905 |
| E. Davidson | 1 May 1905 | 14 May 1919 |
| C. A. Bryant | 15 May 1919 | 17 Jul 1922 |

### Trumpet Majors of the Second Life Guards

| | Appointed | Until |
|---|---|---|
| T. Hopkinson | 2 Dec 1799 | 16 Nov 1802 |
| J. G. Mallick | 17 Nov 1802 | 1805 |
| J. Rivett | 1805 | Aug 1814 |
| W. Body | Aug 1814 | Jun 1816 |
| J. Rawlins Regt. No. 1 | 1 Jul 1816 | 7 Aug 1834 |
| W. Batley | 13 Aug 1834 | 29 May 1845 |
| J. Rawlins Regt. No. 207 | 11 Jun 1845 | 5 Sep 1857 |
| W. J. Cubis | 16 Sep 1857 | 26 Jul 1871 |
| H. J. Furber | Jul 1871 | 25 Mar 1874 |
| G. J. Rawlins | 25 Mar 1874 | 18 Jul 1879 |
| O. C. Woodhouse | 6 Aug 1879 | 11 Jan 1882 |
| W. Stevens | 15 Feb 1882 | 8 Apr 1885 |
| J. J. Barrett | 9 Apr 1885 | 30 Jun 1893 |
| A. J. W. Keightley | 1 Jul 1893 | 26 Apr 1894 |
| S. J. Goodhall | 26 Apr 1894 | 13 Feb 1912 |
| H. E. Pridmore | 14 Feb 1912 | 25 Dec 1913 |
| T. H. Graves | 25 Dec 1913 | 23 Apr 1920 |
| W. A. Warren | 24 Apr 1920 | 11 Oct 1922 |

On 13 February, 1912, Trumpet Major Samuel J. Goodhall of The Second Life Guards died while serving. He was buried with full military honours at Windsor.

The appointment of Trumpet Major Warren lasted until his discharge on 11 October, 1922, which was almost three months after the amalgamation, but as he did not actively serve in the new regiment he was probably on terminal leave.

### Trumpet Majors of The Life Guards

| | Appointed | Until |
|---|---|---|
| C. A. Bryant | continued 18 Jul 1922 | 23 Jun 1923 |
| H. J. Harman | 24 Jun 1923 | 30 Nov 1930 |
| E. Petty | 1 Dec 1930 | 17 May 1936 |
| K. Woodford | 18 May 1936 | 25 Jun 1939 |
| C. J. Leonard | 26 Jun 1939 | 11 Sept 1945 |
| L. G. Smith | 12 Sep 1945 | 30 Sep 1949 |
| B. J. Clarke | 1 Oct 1949 | 19 Jun 1959 |
| E. G. Madden | 20 Jun 1959 | 31 Mar 1969 |
| L. Downs | 1 Apr 1969 | 2 Nov 1970 |

| D. W. Dodson | 3 Nov 1970 | 26 Nov 1974 |
| A. E. Close | 27 Nov 1974 | 11 Mar 1977 |
| R. J. Fletcher | 12 Mar 1977 | 13 Nov 1978 |
| A. E. Close | 14 Nov 1978 | 8 May 1983 |
| A. P. A. Morris | 9 May 1983 | 31 Dec 1988 |
| I. Graves | 1 Jan 1989 | 31 Mar 1994 |
| P. J. Carson | 1 Apr 1994 | |

*Band Corporal Major*
The first Band Corporal of Horse to wear Corporal Major rank insignia was H. G. Sloane in 1949. Honorary W.O.II rank was granted to the B.C.M. on 14 September, 1960. The subtantive rank of W.O.II was added to the band establishment in 1969 but was not instituted until the appointment of R. A. Walthew in 1972. H. B. Dunsmore was not sufficiently qualified to hold the substantive rank and D. W. Dodson's appointment was as acting B.C.M.

### Band Corporals Major of The Life Guards

| | Rank | Appointed | Until |
|---|---|---|---|
| H. G. Sloane | S.Q.M.C. | 12 Nov 1949 | 12 Mar 1956 |
| B. J. Clarke | S.Q.M.C. | 13 Mar 1956 | 19 Jun 1959 |
| R. F. Kennedy | S.Q.M.C. | 20 Jun 1959 | 31 Nov 1959 |
| B. A. Harman | S.Q.M.C. | 14 Nov 1959 | 8 Jun 1962 |
| E. G. Madden | S.Q.M.C. | 20 Jun 1962 | 31 Mar 1969 |
| H. B. Dunsmore | Staff Cpl. | 17 Dec 1969 | 24 Aug 1972 |
| D. W. Dodson | Staff Cpl. | 24 Aug 1972 | 31 Oct 1972 |
| R. A. Walthew | W.O.II | 1 Nov 1972 | 3 Sep 1977 |
| B. J. Frost | W.O.II | 4 Sep 1977 | 13 Nov 1978 |
| R. J. Fletcher | W.O.II | 14 Nov 1978 | 1 Jan 1983 |
| F. J. Harman | W.O.II | 2 Jan 1983 | 31 Dec 1988 |
| A. P. A. Morris | W.O.II | 1 Jan 1989 | 31 Dec 1991 |
| R. P. Bourne | W.O.II | 1 Jan 1992 | 17 Jan 1993 |
| I. Graves | W.O.II | 18 Jan 1993 | |

# APPENDIX III

# Badges of Rank

Badges of rank are not worn on the full dress tunic of N.C.Os and W.Os of The Life Guards Band, excepting the Trumpet Major. Rank is always shown in full dress by aiguillettes. No rank is shown on State Dress. Chevrons have been and are worn on most other orders of dress.

*Lance Corporals and Corporals*
Stable Jacket:- 2 gold lace chevrons on a blue background surmounted by a gold-embroidered crown, on the right upper sleeve.

Blue Drill/Patrol Jacket:- 2 gold russia chevrons on a blue background surmounted by a gold-embroidered crown, on the right upper sleeve.

Service Dress Jacket:- 2 worsted chevrons on a khaki background surmounted by a brass crown, on both upper sleeves.

Battledress Blouse:- As for service dress.

No. 2 Dress:- As for service dress.

British Warm:- 2 worsted chevrons on both lower sleeves.

Cloak:- 2 sand yellow worsted chevrons on a blue background on the lower right sleeve.

Mess Dress:- 2 gold lace chevrons on a blue background surmounted by a gold-embroidered crown, on the right upper sleeve.

*Corporal of Horse*
Orders of Dress as Listed Above:- As for Lance Corporal and Corporal but with 3 instead of 2 chevrons.

*Squadron Quartermaster Corporal and Staff Corporal*
Blue Patrol Jacket:- 4 gold russia inverted chevrons on a blue background surmounted by a gold-embroidered crown, on the lower right sleeve.

Service Dress Jacket:- 4 worsted inverted chevrons on a khaki background surmounted by a brass crown, worn on both lower sleeves.

Battledress Blouse:- As for service dress.

No. 2 Dress:- As for service dress.

British Warm:- As for service dress.

Cloak:- 4 sand yellow worsted inverted chevrons on a blue background, on the right lower sleeve.

Mess Dress:- 4 gold lace inverted chevrons on a blue background surmounted by a gold-embroidered crown, on the right lower sleeve.

*Band Corporal Major and Assistant Band Corporal Major*
Blue Patrol Jacket:- A gold-embroidered crown within a wreath of laurel leaves on a blue background, on the right lower sleeve.

Service Dress Jacket:- A brass crown within a wreath of laurel leaves on both lower sleeves.

Battledress Blouse:- As for service dress.

No. 2 Dress:- As for service dress.

British Warm:- As for service dress.

Cloak:- A sand yellow embroidered crown within a wreath of laurel leaves on a blue background, on the right lower sleeve.

Mess Dress:- A gold-embroidered crown within a wreath of laurel leaves on a blue background, on the right lower sleeve.

*Lance Corporal of Horse*
Since 1972 the rank of Corporal has been replaced by that of Lance Corporal of Horse, who wears the same rank badges as a Corporal of Horse but substituting a worsted embroidered crown for the brass crown worn by the Corporal of Horse. Some corporals were appointed L/CoH as early as 1970 and in these early days wore a brass crown.

During the Second World War worsted embroidered crowns were worn on battledress by all band N.C.Os.

The appointment of Trumpet Major is held by a Corporal, Corporal of Horse, Staff Corporal or Corporal Major. If he is of the first three ranks he wears the rank badges as described for a Squadron Quartermaster-Corporal or Staff Corporal but with the addition of crossed trumpets of the same material as the crown, below which they are worn. If the Trumpet Major is also the B.C.M. or A.B.C.M. he wears the badges of that rank with crossed trumpets of the same material below. Before 1978 crossed trumpets were worn on the right sleeve only; since then they have been worn on both sleeves of No. 2 Dress. Crossed trumpets are not worn on the British Warm or cloak.

On the full dress tunic the Trumpet Major of The Life Guards, irrespective of rank, wears a large gold-embroidered crown above crossed trumpets, all on a blue background, on the lower right sleeve as was the custom in the First Life Guards. The Trumpet Major of the Second Life Guards wore the same insignia but on the upper right sleeve.

On stable dress of the mid-nineteenth century, the Trumpet Major of the First Regiment wore 4 chevrons of 1-inch-wide gold lace surmounted by gold-embroidered crossed trumpets on a blue background, in about 1874 a gold-embroidered crown was added. These were worn on the upper right sleeve. His counterpart in the Second Regiment wore 4 chevrons of 5/8-inch-wide gold lace surmounted by a gold-embroidered crown, all on a blue background, on the upper right sleeve; he did not wear crossed trumpets. From 1886 the Trumpet Major of the the Second Regiment wore 4 inverted chevrons of 5/8-inch-wide gold lace surmounted by gold-embroidered crossed trumpets and a crown, on the lower right sleeve.

From 1992, on the orders of the Major General, the Band Corporal Major wore a gold-embroidered crown within a wreath of laurel leaves on a blue background, on the lower right sleeve of his full dress scarlet tunic. This was discontinued in January, 1994.

# APPENDIX IV

# Principal Players

Listed here are some of the principal players of the bands. It has not been possible to name many of the earlier players as service records do not give details of instruments. In most cases the dates given are approximate. Also listed are pianists and players of string instruments who were mostly of the nineteen-fifties era.

## FIRST LIFE GUARDS

### Flute

| | | | |
|---|---|---|---|
| Sheppard | 1890 | Hall | 1902 |
| J. C. Barber | −1902 | | |

### Eb Clarinet

| | |
|---|---|
| J. Carter | 1905 |

### Oboe

| | | | |
|---|---|---|---|
| H. Henton | 1870 | D. F. Griffiths | 1920 |
| Bond | 1901 | | |

### Bb Clarinet

| | | | |
|---|---|---|---|
| J. Waterson | 1853–63 | W. M. Hopkins | 1890–98 |
| J. Style | 1863 | | |

### Bassoon

| | | | |
|---|---|---|---|
| J. Wight | 1860 | J. Gerella | 1908–10 |
| W. B. Wotton | 1860–67 | H. E. J. Moore | 1910–14 |
| Francis | 1895 | | |

### Cornet

| | | | |
|---|---|---|---|
| Fenwick | 1895 | J. Raine | 1915 |
| Morgan | 1910 | Jones | 1919 |

*Trombone*

W. Winterbottom     1840–53

*Euphonium*

A. Cousins                       C. A. Bryant     1915–22
A. E. Bannister    1895–97

## SECOND LIFE GUARDS

*Oboe*

E. Crozier         1865          J. McCarthy     1918–22

*Bb Clarinet*

H. E. Pridmore    –1913        G. Pipe         –1922

*Bassoon*

P. J. Keenan     –1922

*Cornet*

H. N. Harman    1915–22

*Horn*

A. J. W. Keightley  1878–94     W. R. Urwin     1909–19

*Trombone*

E. Adams        1905–07

*Euphonium*

W. A. Warren    –1922

*Percussion*

J. E. Hanrahan   –1914       W. J. Grace     1914–22

## THE LIFE GUARDS

*Flute*

| G. McBride | 1926–28 | R. A. Ely | 1974–77 |
| R. G. Thornburrow | 1937–45 | K. Meikle | 1977–79 |
| N. Sleigh | 1948–52 | C. Kidd | 1979–83 |
| D. J. Banger | 1952–55 | F. Poland | 1983–88 |
| H. P. N. Steinitz | 1958–61 | K. A. Pearson | 1988– |
| A. W. Hocking | 1961–74 | | |

## Eb Clarinet

| | | | |
|---|---|---|---|
| E. Petty | –1936 | J. P. Walthew | 1962–63 |
| J. Mantle | 1937–45 | A. Johnson | 1963–65 |
| F. Bowden | 1945–56 | B. J. Frost | 1965–74 |
| A. Woodhead | 1956–62 | F. J. Campbell | 1974–76 |

## Oboe

| | | | |
|---|---|---|---|
| S. Smith | 1930 | I. Graham | 1966–71 |
| E. Batty | 1945–53 | A. P. A. Morris | 1971–91 |
| P. Jones | 1953–57 | M. J. Hopkins | 1991–92 |
| D. W. B. Singleton | 1957–66 | D. A. Smart | 1992– |

## Bb Clarinet

| | | | |
|---|---|---|---|
| L. Hazell | | C. F. Parr | 1959–63 |
| K. Woodford | 1939–41 | J. P. Walthew | 1963–64 |
| L. Hazell | 1941–45 | R. A. Walthew | 1964–65 |
| D. P. O'Donovan | 1945 | J. P. Walthew | 1965–70 |
| W. G. Hambleton | 1945–48 | R. A. Walthew | 1970–77 |
| F. E. Perks | 1948–53 | B. J. Frost | 1977–79 |
| J. Denman | 1953–55 | D. J. Mean | 1979–89 |
| D. O'Connor | 1955–59 | P. D. Lazenbury | 1989– |

## Bassoon

| | | | |
|---|---|---|---|
| H. E. Sloane | 1935–56 | K. R. Whitworth | 1971–88 |
| T. W. Thompson | 1956–58 | G. Chiverton | 1988–89 |
| H. J. Robb | 1959–69 | G. J. Semkin | 1989– |

## Alto Saxophone

| | | | |
|---|---|---|---|
| W. Jordan | 1935–39 | R. F. Kennedy | 1949–65 |
| E. Ineson | 1939–40 | G. Taylor | 1965–78 |
| G. Henley | 1940–45 | M. J. Hopkins | 1978–91 |
| J. Cox | 1945–49 | O. N. Gook | 1991– |

## Tenor Saxophone

| | | | |
|---|---|---|---|
| E. Metcalfe | 1924–35 | R. P. Bourne | 1980–82 |
| R. F. Kennedy | 1939–49 | O. N. Gook | 1982–84 |
| I. D. Gunn | 1949–56 | R. P. Bourne | 1984–93 |
| D. W. Dodson | 1956–74 | N. L. Maher | 1993– |
| R. S. Hart | 1974–80 | | |

## Baritone Saxophone

| | | | |
|---|---|---|---|
| R. P. Bourne | 1974–80 | O. N. Gook | 1984–87 |
| R. P. Bourne | 1982–84 | | |

### French Horn

| | | | |
|---|---|---|---|
| J. Mason | 1922– | A. E. Close | 1968–70 |
| J. Buck | 1940–45 | R. T. Barnes | 1970–81 |
| N. Sanders | 1945–46 | A. E. Close | 1981–83 |
| R. Powell | 1946–51 | M. Collier | 1983–87 |
| W. H. Chessman | 1951–68 | I. J. Stott | 1987– |

### Cornet

| | | | |
|---|---|---|---|
| H. J. Harman | 1925–30 | W. Marsden | 1972–83 |
| Franklin | 1930– | R. M. Young | 1983–84 |
| C. J. Leonard | 1939–45 | I. Graves | 1984– |
| H. B. Dunsmore | 1945–72 | | |

### Trombone

| | | | |
|---|---|---|---|
| L. Woodford | 1930–37 | C. T. Dean | 1971–77 |
| R. L. B. Garbutt | 1937–41 | J. A. Nicholls | 1977–78 |
| J. H. Ashby | 1941–45 | P. B. Fenson | 1978–79 |
| R. L. B. Garbutt | 1945 | I. Bromley | 1979–89 |
| W. J. C. J. W. Cross | 1945–64 | M. Grieve | 1989 |
| C. Messenger | 1964–68 | J. Field | 1989– |
| D. Halstead | 1968–71 | | |

### Euphonium

| | | | |
|---|---|---|---|
| C. A. Bryant | 1922–23 | A. P. Legge | 1964–77 |
| A. Cawdery | 1930–45 | D. M. Bole | 1977–87 |
| H. A. R. V. White | 1945–48 | J. H. Morrish | 1987–89 |
| White | 1948–49 | D. M. Bole | 1989– |
| P. Ravenor | 1949–64 | | |

### Bass

| | | | |
|---|---|---|---|
| R. E. Croxon | 1930–49 | P. R. Manfield | 1973–80 |
| G. Williams | 1949–52 | R. J. Fletcher | 1980–83 |
| R. McDonald | 1952–68 | B. Cox | 1984–90 |
| M. Lucas | 1968–73 | A. K. Walsh | 1990– |

### Percussion

| | | | |
|---|---|---|---|
| W. J. Grace | 1922–24 | G. R. Lawn | 1962–65 |
| G. Carter | 1924–27 | E. G. Madden | 1965–69 |
| F. C. Hodgkins | 1928–36 | F. J. Harman | 1969–88 |
| N. Harris | 1936–45 | G. Dare | 1988 |
| W. Connor | 1945–50 | S. J. Bolstridge | 1988–94 |
| H. Cardell | 1950–53 | J. Mathews | 1994– |
| B. A. Harman | 1953–62 | | |

*String Players who served with the Band between 1939 and 1970*

## Violin

| | | | |
|---|---|---|---|
| M. Bebb | 1957–60 | N. Nelson | 1949–51 |
| T. Colman | 1966–69 | R. J. Ovens | 1952–55 |
| A. Cleveland | 1949–50 | A. J. Peters | 1955–58 |
| J. G. Davies | 1952–55 | K. Sillito | 1958–60 |
| M. Henderson | 1953–57 | D. Solomons | 1959–62 |
| B. Hill | 1955–58 | A. Traverse | 1956–61 |
| D. Houston | 1951–54 | B. Townsend | 1959–62 |
| M. Latcham | 1949–50 | L. Ullman | 1957–60 |
| L. Lewis | 1953–56 | S. L. Wicebloom | 1949–51 |
| L. McManson | 1942–45 | J. Willison | 1955–58 |
| B. Miller | 1957–60 | J. R. M. Woolf MBE | 1949–51 |

Two former Life Guards violinists have since been honoured. John Woolf was made a MBE in 1974 for services to music for his work with The Park Lane Group and the Society For The Promotion of New Music. Derek Solomons, for services to Italian music, was in 1980 awarded the Cavaliere al Merito della Repubblica Italiana.

## Viola

| | | | |
|---|---|---|---|
| G. P. Bolgar | 1958–61 | F. Muller | 1952–55 |
| J. Cummings | 1957–59 | B. Tasker | 1955–57 |

## Cello

| | | | |
|---|---|---|---|
| A. F. Dalziel | 1952–55 | P. C. Vel | 1958–60 |
| J. H. A. Stillwell | 1955–58 | | |

*Pianists who served between 1940 and 1965*

| | | | |
|---|---|---|---|
| H. Parr-Davies | 1941–46 | B. Booth | 1958–61 |
| A. Monaghan | 1946–56 | G. Wells | 1961–64 |
| E. G. Aitken | 1949–52 | A. Johnson | 1963–65 |
| J. R. Constable | 1954–57 | | |

# Index